Welcome to the 10th edition of Itchy. Whe[ther] you're an Itchy virgin or an old flame, we'[re] here to help you make the most of going o[ut] in Birmingham. We hope you enjoy yoursel[ves] as much as we have over the last 10 years.

GW01072055

IN-HOUSE TEAM

Editor: Mike Toller
Local editor: Joly Braime
Features editor: Alexi Duggins
Editorial and production assistants:
Clare Cullen, Alix Fox
Editorial assistants: Jon Lynes, Anton Tweedale
Editorial assistance: Iliana Dracou, Sam Shields, Achmed Esser, Cory Burdette, Lily Gorlin, Rozanne Gelbinovich, Maisie McCabe, Julie Dyer, Jackie Fishman
Designers: Paul Jones, Sara Gramner
Design assistance: Katelyn Boller
Picture research: Tiago Genoveze, Philip Kelly, Neha Bhargava, Katelyn Boller
Production consultant: Iain Leslie
National ad sales: Sue Ostler, Zee Ahmad
Local ad sales: Catherine Farinha
Distribution: Efua Hagan
Financial controller: Sharon Watkins
Managing director: Ian Merricks
Publisher: Itchy Group
© 2008 Itchy Group
ISBN: 978-1-905705-26-9

BIRMINGHAM TEAM

City editor: Ruth Wright

Contributors: Tess Langley, Ifunanya Ifeacho, Aaron Wright, Dale Kedwards, Michelle Wilson, Dominic Stanley, Lydia Johnson, Ian Cassidy, Gemma Boland, Simone de la Fuente, James Hassell, Claire Samuel, Dame Amy

Photography: Mike Hale, Lydia Unsworth, Roland Eva, Tiago Genoveze, Rosie Kelly, Sarah Morecombe, Juliet Hookey, Selma Yalazi Dawani, Chriss Grossmeier

Cover and feature illustrations: www.si-clark.co.uk

Itchy Group
78 Liverpool Road, London, N1 0QD
Tel: 020 7288 9810
Fax: 020 7288 9815
E-mail: editor@itchymedia.co.uk
Web: www.itchycity.co.uk

Itchy ➔
Contents

Contents

Introduction

Welcome to Birmingham

BIG, BOLD, BADASS, BRUM.

Happy birthday to us, happy birthday to us, happy birthday dear u-us, happy birthday to us. We can hardly believe it's been 10 years since we first opened our pages to the sights and sounds of good ol' Brummywood, this Mecca of the Midlands. But don't worry, we're not quite ready for the knacker's yard just yet (and when we do get sent down, we're taking you with us). We're still brimming with excitement at all things Birmingham. Oh, for the buzz of the Bullring, the brilliance of the Birmingham Repertory Theatre, and the bright lights of Broad Street. Although, now we're all grown up we hit the trendy bars at the Mailbox and try to pass ourselves off as sophisticated. All thoughts of refinement leave our head at the very mention of Cadbury World (even if we didn't get to punch Mr Cadbury's parrot like we'd hoped). So, let's all take a deep breath as we plunge headlong into the UK's second city (you'll always be first to us, Brum).

Changes in Brum over the last ten years

THE LAST TEN YEARS HAVE SEEN BIRMINGHAM BOOM AND THANK GOD FOR THAT. 'INDUSTRIAL' AND 'MONSTROSITY' ARE LONG GONE AS THE BUZZ WORDS, REPLACED BY 'MODERN', 'CULTURAL' AND 'CADBURY'S', A FACTORY OF JOY WHICH HAS REALLY PUT THIS PLACE ON THE MAP. LAST YEAR 30 MILLION VISITORS CAME TO SEE WHY WE'RE THE SECOND CITY AND, JUDGING BY THE STREET-CLEANING BILL, WE'D SAY THEY HAD A PRETTY GOOD TIME.

Jewellery, guns and related metal goodies are Brum's traditional stock-in-trade, but suits of armour just don't sell like they used to, so we've moved on to the material kind. In fact, the Association for Pointless Statistics tells us that women in Birmingham spend more on fashion than any other UK city. The Bullring, Selfridges and the Mailbox now provide a walk-in wardrobe to rival Imelda Marcos'.

The Bullring has been grabbing Brummies by the cojones for over 40 years; but the last ten have seen it go from trashy to classy, like a Britney in reverse. Pop imagery aside, the revamp transformed the shopping district, and the centre is now the busiest in the country, making Christmas shopping an unrivalled joy (sort of).

If clothes don't cling to you like culture does, Birmingham's got it covered. The West End is child's play compared to Brum's sophisticated theatre scene, and the brand spanking new Town Hall is a worthy addition. After a quarter of a century serving the city, some smart Spencer decided it was in need of a well-earned rest and revamp, so in 1996 after they channelled the equivalent of a footballer's weekly earnings into it, one of the best new venues in the country was born. From footballers to their wannabe wives, Broad Street is to clubbing what Posh is to laxatives: highly dependent.

Changes are coming thick and fast in other parts of the city too, with re-development plans for Digbeth and Eastside up next. So whether it's food, music, art or gay cabaret that gives you a tingle, Birmingham is well-equipped to oblige.

On the downside, our status as the strip club capital of England is a rare low point for most of us (unless you are one of those with a penchant for paying to see ladies take their clothes off), but at least it's generating commerce for our fair city. Every cloud has a silver lining, and all that. So whistle while you read this, friends, and book yourself a ticket to Brum, or if you're already a local, buy yourself a bus pass and get cracking. There's plenty to see...

Top five places to have your photo taken

Hire a bull from a local farmer and pose with it next to the replica by the Bullring. You'll be the envy of every tourist in town.

Find one of the many houses raided for suicide bombers and pose in the front garden.

Go down to the Birmingham City ground wearing a Villa shirt and have your photo taken with a friendly Blues fan.

Climb the Selfridges building and get a friend to document the arrest.

Motorway fans can take their pick of any one of the city's flyovers for a stunning picture to add to their 'UK roads' collection.

Local Lingo

OWAMYA?=HOW ARE YOU? YOW NO MI BAB?=HAVE YOU MET MY FRIEND BEFORE? ARSE CREAM=FROZEN CONFECTIONERY. WE AM ON WE OLIDAZE=WE'RE ON OUR HOLIDAYS. UP THE WOODEN HILL=UPSTAIRS. TRARAABIT=SEE YOU SOON. MOI=MONTH BEFORE JUNE OR INDICATING POSSESSION OF SOMETHING. KINNOY=CAN I? MOWTA=CAR. TITTYBABBI=PERSON ACTING IMMATURELY, LIKE A BABY, SUCKLING.

Quirky facts

The Rough Guide ranks Birmingham as a more desirable place to live than Rome, Milan or Barcelona.

The inspiration for *Thomas the Tank Engine* came from Kings Norton Station.

Robert Plant was added to the Led Zeppelin line-up after Jimmy Page saw him play a gig in Brum's own Selly Oak.

The first X-Ray was done in Birmingham.

During Victorian times Birmingham was known as the pen shop of the world, and was making 28 million pen nibs per week.

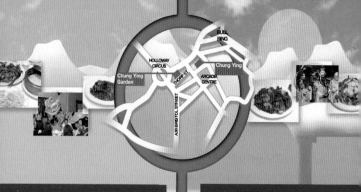

中英花園飯店
CHUNG YING GARDEN
Cantonese Restaurant

中英大飯店
CHUNG YING
Cantonese Restaurant

17 THORP STREET,
BIRMINGHAM, B5 4AT
TELEPHONE: 0121 666 6622
FAX: 0121 622 5860

16-18 WROTTESLEY STREET
BIRMINGHAM, B5 4RT
TELEPHONE: 0121 622 1793
FAX: 0121 666 7051

EMAIL: CHUNGYINGGARDEN@AOL.COM
WWW.CHUNGYING.CO.UK

EMAIL: CHUNGYING@AOL.COM
WWW.CHUNGYING.CO.UK

We are 25 years old!

Karaoke and disco available (CYG only)

Dlicious cantonese food

Extensive traditional menu

the original name in china town

Recommended by the AA & Good Food Guides

Eat

Eat

We've got so many Michelin stars, we might as well adopt the Stars and Stripes as our flag. In fact, we'd say we've got some of the best restaurants in the country, which makes for very happy eating. The main areas for good grub in the city centre are in Brindleyplace, though you'll have to cough up the cash to eat here. The Clubbers' mile is also home to the best Sunday roast in town. **The Brasshouse (44 Broad Street, 0121 633 3383)** offers big portions, cosy corners and real ales to wash it all down. **The Living Room (Unit 4, Regency Wharf 2, Broad Street, 0870 442 2539)** is the perfect people-watching spot as it overlooks Broad Street, but isn't too high up to make you feel queasy. Their Sunday brunch isn't cheap, but the best hangover cures always come at a price. Finally if you're a veggie or vegan about town, **Sibila's (Canal Square, Browning Street, 0121 456 7634)** is a must-go for very creative cooking and organic cider to boot.

Top five cheap eats
Urban Pie – Best pie under the Brum sky.
Handmade Burger Co – Cheap as the chunky chips on the side.
Big Wok – Enough to feed a small Chinatown.
Rooty Frooty – Even hippies have to eat sometimes.
Café One – They're more creative with their food than their name.

Top five places for a posh meal
Opus – Food too beautiful to touch, so have a sarnie beforehand.
Nathaniel's – About as big as your kitchen, but with much better results.
Pennyblacks – Won't break the bank, will get you in her/his pants.
The Living Room – Not actually like your lounge at home.
Bank – Ker-ching.

The Balti Triangle

UNLIKE ITS SHIP-SWALLOWING NAMESAKE, THE BALTI TRIANGLE IS JUST SOUTH OF THE CITY CENTRE AND THE ONLY PLACE TO GO FOR AN AUTHENTIC BALTI CURRY. AFTER YEARS OF EATING CURRY IN BRUM, WE'D SAY THE TRIANGLE IS SOMEWHERE BETWEEN SPARKHILL, SPARKBROOK AND MOSELEY. IF YOU'RE SUDDENLY BLINDED, YOU'VE HIT IT. FLASHING NEON SIGNS TRY TO LURE YOU IN BUT TO SAVE YOU HAVING TO TURN DOWN 50 ANGRY WAITERS, WE THOUGHT WE'D HELP YOU OUT. OUR GUIDE WILL ACT AS A SPOON ON YOUR TONGUE AND LEAD YOU TO THE TASTIEST TANDOORIS. BETTER STILL, ALL OF OUR FAVOURITES ARE 'BRING YOUR OWN', WITH OFF-LICENCES A MINUTE'S WALK AWAY.

First up is **Al Frash**. Poncy food critics rave about it, and rightly so. It's just amazing. Absolutely everything on the huge menu is worth having, and at the prices they charge, that might not seem like such a bad idea. **Jewel in the Crown** has everything you need for a classic curry house: tacky décor, big portions and late opening hours, making it the best post-pub option for a poppadom or two. **Plaza** wouldn't win a beauty pageant, but it's a firm favourite for picky eaters; if you can't hack the spice, they'll make it how you like it. Herbivores, hold your carrot sticks, we haven't forgotten you. **Jyoti** is your spiritual home in the triangle with every dish lovely and veggie, or even vegan. Chicken korma shmorma, we say.

Finally, a hot tip, literally. If your mouth is on fire and you can't take the heat, don't ask for a glass of water, as this will make it worse. Yoghurt is a much better cooler.

Al Frash
186 Ladypool Road, Sparkbrook, (0121) 753 3120
🕐 Mon–Sun, 5pm–late; take-out available 24 hours

Jewel in the Crown
125 Alcester Road, Moseley, (0121) 449 4335
🕐 Sun–Thu, 6pm–12am; Fri-Sat, 6pm–1am

Plaza
278 Ladypool Road, Sparkbrook, (0121) 449 4249
🕐 Mon–Sun, 5pm–12am

Jyoti
569-571 Stratford Road, Sparkhill, (0121) 766 7199
🕐 Tue & Wed, 6pm–9.30pm; Thu–Sun, 1pm–3pm & 6pm–9.30pm

Eat

CAFÉS

Arts Café
St Martin's, Bullring
(0121) 643 5428

Part of pretty St Martin's church, you might associate this little eatery more closely with religion than arts, but maybe they're branching out. They do a full English in the morning, and sandwiches with Italian names for lunch, while those into humanitarian nutrition can be smug in the knowledge that most ingredients are Fairtrade, and profits go to St Martin's. The churches of St Nero's and St Starbucks just opposite don't do quite the same good work.

🕑 *Tue–Sat, 10am–3pm*
🍴 *Pasta in arrabbiata sauce with side salad, £5.50*

Café Jouel
72 Vyse Street, Hockley
(0121) 551 6991

Once you've had your fill of men in costumes and enough sparkle to last a lifetime in the Jewellery Quarter Museum, head next door for a more matte finish. Big comfy sofas or arty bamboo contraptions provide varying degrees of comfort for your weary bones. Painted canvasses by local artists have saved them a ton on wallpaper too. Just avoid the café on weekday lunchtimes when it's swamped by office workers tucking into the exceptional 'BBC' sandwich. That's brie, bacon and cheddar by the way, unfortunately not the innards of popular TV personalities.

🕑 *Tue–Sat, 9.15am–4pm*
🍴 *BBC sandwich, £4.50*

Beams Creperie
The Pallasades
(07917) 626 618

Expert tossers these folk at Beams Creperie, but thankfully in a very good way. They've got a flipping good selection of sweet and savoury crepes, made right in front of your very eyes. You'll soon realise that when a pint's not an option, a crepe and a generous scoop of chocolate ice cream are just the ticket for those days when things just don't seem to be going your way. Sure it's not exactly gourmet fare, but it's not total crepe either, and it's much batter for you than a burger. It's cheap and cheerful, and that's bound to get you beaming.

🕑 *Mon–Sat, 8am–7pm; Sun, 9.30am–5pm*
🍴 *Lemon and sugar crepe, £3.10*

Café One
Five Ways
(0121) 245 0001

One of Brum's best cafés is hidden away amongst derelict clubs and bars by the Five Ways roundabout. The emphasis on fair and ethical trade could put off the narrow-minded, but those of small cranium miss out on original food, good tunes and lovely people. A couple of big square tables fill up the space and make mingling obligatory on their music nights. The buffet lunch provides great value and is more like a home-cooked meal than mass catering.

🕑 *Mon–Fri, 8.30am–3.30pm;*
Thu–Sat, 5pm–late
🍴 *All-you-can-eat buffet, lunch, £3.95; evening, £5.95*
💰 *£7*

Café Soya II

Unit 2, Upper Dean Street

(0121) 622 3888

Sister branch to number one in the Arcadian, the Vietnamese cuisine includes noodles, soups, spice, and soya. You can't really get away from the wonder protein – it's in more or less everything, and you ain't leaving 'til you've tried it. Though only a small part of the menu is meat-free, their cunning fake chicken can be substituted in all the other meat dishes. This stuff looks just like the real thing and is as tasty as real flesh, but is made from, umm.. soya. Big, bright and busy, so they must be doing something right. Soya, perhaps?

🕒 *Mon–Sun, 12pm–11pm*
🍴 *Papaya salad vermicelli, £8.90*
💷 *£9.95*

The Hylton Café

2 Hylton Street, Hockley

(0121) 554 005

A typical British café with sweet little grannies in floral aprons tottering around holding precariously-balanced trays of tea. Ours'll be tea with milk and two sugars, and the sexiest, greasiest burger to be found this side of Albert Square. It sounds pleasingly like it might be associated with the hotel chain, but lacks the refinement of its namesake, with everything sort of flung onto your plate then drowned beyond recognition in a generous side-slopping of ketchup. The toilet's in a separate outbuilding, so a quick jog to the bog will soon shift the pounds you've just piled on.

🕒 *Mon–Fri, 7am–2.30pm; Sat, 8am–2.30pm*
🍴 *Sexy cheese burger and chips, £3.55*

Gordon Blue

53 Frederick Street, Jewellery Quarter

(0121) 693 2345

Okay, so it's a bit weird to classify cappuccino and latte on your menu as 'posh coffees' nowadays. Still, when you offer a bacon buttie and steaming, sugary tea for less than an over-frothed milky mixture in a cardboard cup, you can afford to be a bit Jurassic. With hot, cold and tepid treats to feed you from breakfast 'til afternoon tea, they've got every hunger pang covered. With a loyal lunchtime crowd who could make the journey here from their office blindfolded, in this part of town they don't need cordon bleu when they can sample a little Gordon Blue.

🕒 *Mon–Fri, 7am–3.30pm; Sat, 9am–3.30pm*
🍴 *All day breakfast, £2.90*

Kitchen Garden Café

17 York Road, Kings Heath

(0121) 443 4725

Suburban mothers rejoice, this all-in-one café, deli, garden shop and restaurant is dedicated to the middle class raison d'être: organic produce. Set in an old brick courtyard, it's like finding a café in a hidden corner of the secret garden. Veggies and children are very well taken care of, and you can buy the ingredients at the deli as you leave. So what with the seats being at the back, no-one need know about that hemp beer, meaning that this organic business isn't all just sweetness and light.

🕒 *Mon–Wed, 9.30am–5pm; Thu–Sat,*
9.30am–5pm & 7pm–11.30pm;
Sun, 10am–3.30pm
🍴 *Moroccan lamb with tabouleh, £12.95*

Eat

Pete's Café

52–53 Warstone Lane, Hockley
(0121) 212 0250

Having decided to open a food establishment in the Jewellery Quarter, it seems Pete couldn't decide what type of food he should serve. So, to make things easier, he just threw all his eggs (and chips, sausages, bacon, tuna, ham, curry, jacket potatoes, etc.) into one massive basket, and decided to serve everything. This resulted in a greasy spoon/fish 'n' chip restaurant/sandwich bar all rolled into one. Precious few marks for presentation, but Pete does churn out enough varieties of fast food to feed the world ten times over. Sweaty cook with hairnet included.

🕐 *Mon–Fri, 8am–9pm; Sat, 8am–6pm*
🍴 *Full English, £3.90*

Warehouse Café

54–57 Allison Street,
Digbeth
(0121) 633 0261

Visiting the Warehouse Café is a bit like going round to your hippy mate's flat. The veggie café is on the first floor of Birmingham's Friends of the Earth building, so you know you're not in for a microwaved Big Mac. Solar panels heat their water and used vegetable oil becomes fuel for a car that actually runs. The cheap, simple, but very filling food changes daily. Homemade cake and tea for afters complete the perfect meal, wherever you sit on the food chain.

🕐 *Mon–Sat, 11am–10pm; Sun, 11am–6pm*
🍴 *Mushroom sausages with roast garlic, parsley mash and wild mushrooms, £7.65*
🍷 *BYO*

Sibila's at Body and Being

Canal Square, Browning Street
(0121) 456 7634

Right next door to a health spa and serving up only vegetarian and organic food, it's a café by day and a restaurant by night. Maybe not the most cosy or romantic of settings, but cares like these fly out the window once you're served. Even Picasso wasn't as creative as the chefs at Sibila. Tasty, wholesome, colourful and eye-opening. And that's just the waitresses. Even the most stubborn of carnivores will have a hard time fighting their corner.

🕐 *Mon, 12pm–3pm; Tue–Fri, 12pm–3pm & 6pm–10pm; Sat, 6pm–10pm; Sun, 12.30pm–4pm*
🍴 *Buffet lunch, £5.99*
🍷 *£9.90*

Urban Pie

Bullring

(0121) 643 0040

At a glance, 'gourmet pies' is one of those weird contradictions in terms; not unlike 'the living dead', 'awfully nice', 'Postal Service' or 'American English'. At Urban Pie, however, 'gourmet' meets 'pie' wonderfully – and the result has very little in common with any of the above. It's good, wholesome food that's not fussy or complicated. Those nice-as-pie chappies will even deliver direct to your work or home. Hide the packaging and you can easily convince friends or relatives that you too can cook this well. Marks out of five? Itchy gives it 3.142... Geddit?

☻ Mon–Sun, 10am–8pm

🍴 Lamb and rosemary pie, £2.65

RESTAURANTS

Bank

4 Brindleyplace

(0121) 633 4466

With awards adorning their walls, Bank don't really need another glowing review. So we'll get the compliments out the way. The food is among the best in Birmingham. Try as we may, we can't knock it. The uniforms and lighting, however, are ripe for a swipe. The waiters' suits should be destroyed and talking is a chore under the glare of the lighting. Table for one, please.

☻ Mon–Fri, 7.30am–10.30am, 12pm–3pm & 5.30pm–11pm (Fri, 11.30pm); Sat, 11.30am–3pm; Sun, 11.30am–3.30pm & 5pm–10pm

🍴 Sausage and mash with gravy, £11.75

✪ £12.95

Woodstock

584 Bristol Road, Selly Oak

(0121) 471 4050

Crosby, Stills and Nash haven't turned up yet, but young students fill this café. The bohemian spirit of its namesake haunts the folky soundtrack and every-man-for-himself attitude to seating. But don't be fooled, their menu's a serious affair. Just choosing the bread for your sandwich is a difficult task, never mind the filling. It's been around longer than most of the mad professors at the campus across the road and practice has made perfect. Good grub cheap enough to fill that hole in your beans-on-toast-twice-daily diet.

☻ Mon–Fri, 9.30am–7.30pm; Sat, 11.30am–7.30pm; Sun, 11.30am–7pm;

🍴 Mexican special ciabatta, £3.10

Bar Estilo

110–114 Wharfside Street, The Mailbox

(0121) 643 3443

Mexican-themed tapas bar where you're shunted around like cattle then pushed out the gates before the next herd arrives. The tapas is tasty enough, but about as exotic as the sombreros hanging from the walls. The long bar in the middle looks swish but you become a little like goldfish in a bowl if you sit at it, so they tend to rush fresh guests straight to a table, even if the last lot have barely paid their bill. It's fine for a quick dinner, but you should head further into the Mailbox if you're out to impress.

☻ Mon–Sat, 12pm–11pm; Sun, 12pm–10.30pm

🍴 Tapas, £2.95–£5.50 each

✪ £14.95

Eat

Big Wok

5 Wrottesley Street

(0121) 666 6800

For those of you not as well versed as Itchy in the peculiarities of Oriental dialect, 'bigwok' is colloquial Chinese for 'bloody good grub 'n' lots of it'. It is derived from the Mandarin verb 'to wok' meaning 'to gorge oneself to within seconds of falling unconscious on tempura, prawn crackers, chow mein, and up to 60 other dishes'. Should you want to 'bigwok', the Big Wok is, surprisingly, the only place for it. For less than a fiver before 5pm, and less than £9 'til closing time, it can't be beaten on value either. Big wok? It's freakin' monstrous.

🕒 *Mon–Sat, 12pm–11.30pm; Sun, 12pm–11.30pm*

💲 *£8.90*

Casa Lamisa

7 Fletchers Walk, Paradise Place

(0121) 233 1533

The best value Spanish restaurant in Brum. The set menu includes soup, six tapas dishes which change weekly, and dessert. Wash it down with a jug of sangría and you've got yourself a very tasty meal. Tucked away behind the Conservatoire in a dingy stretch of shops, its location might be a bit off-putting, but get inside and it's as warm and cosy as an Ugg boot. With friendly staff and great service, you really can't fault the place. They even have a take-out service, aptly named Dial-a-Spanish.

🕒 *Mon–Thu, 12pm–3pm & 5pm–10pm; Fri–Sat, 12pm–3pm & 5pm–10.30pm*

🍴 *Set menu, £10.50*

💲 *£10.50*

Brasshouse

44 Broad Street

(0121) 633 3383

Any address containing the words 'Broad Street' is generally a big fat warning sign for cheese, chavs and chunder. Brasshouse is an exception to the rule. Cheese is confined to the kitchen, a strict but fair door policy keeps out the Kappa crew, and they wisely refuse to serve anyone close to the vomiting stage. While their selection of real ales is impressive, their Sunday lunch is legendary. Our stomach's rumbling just at the thought.

🕒 *Mon–Thu, 11.30am–11pm; Fri–Sat, 11.30am–2am; Sun, 12pm–10.30pm; food, Mon–Sat, 12pm–9pm; Sun, 12pm–5pm*

🍴 *Sunday carvery, £7.50*

💲 *£7.50*

Chez Jules

5a Ethel Street

(0121) 633 4664

Chez Jules tries to bring simple French cooking to Brum, but given how complex the dishes on the menu sound, you could fool us. Still, they deserve kudos for the rustic décor, as well as hiring real French staff in the Gallic vacuum of Birmingham. Still, this doesn't mean you should expect a gastoronomic revolution, as the food's fairly unremarkable. Then again, with two courses for £10.95 and a romantic ambience, it's hard to complain. Plus the food's nicely unpretentious, which is rare for the French.

🕒 *Mon–Sat, 12pm–4pm & 5pm–11pm; Sun, 12pm–6pm*

🍴 *Char grilled rib eye steak, £12.95*

Cuizene

29 Edgbaston Shopping Centre
(0121) 454 9257

The hot buffet in this bright Caribbean restaurant has a good selection of meat, rice and fish dishes with a twist, and plenty of vegetarian options as well. The 'twist' can be pretty spicy, so don't be shy to ask what you're getting first. The very friendly staff will be happy to tell you every ingredient, and probably where it's grown too, just in case you're into that kind of thing. If you're short on time, weigh 'n' pay or eat in, where we promise ya will nah leave without ya belly full, man.

☻ *Mon–Thu, 11.30am–3pm; Fri, 7pm–11pm;*
Sat, 6.30pm–11pm
🍴 *Buffet, £4.49; weigh 'n' pay, 79p/100g*
🍷 *BYO*

Chung Ying Garden

17 Thorp Street
(0121) 666 6622

Big sister to original China Town big hitter Chung Ying, Chung Ying Garden has no less than 450 dishes to dribble, drool and slobber over. This includes a vast array of set banquets, and live seafood too, so those whose cockles are warmed by the thought of eating briny beasts fresh from the tank will be squids in. Even with the enormous range of choices on offer, the CYG kitchen have had their repertoire down pat since 1987, and everything Itchy has ever ordered has been delicious, delightful, delovely.

☻ *Mon–Sat, 12pm–11.30pm;*
Sun, 12pm–10.30pm
🍴 *Steamed eel in black bean sauce, £12*
🍷 *£12.95*

Chung Ying

16–18 Wrottesley Street
(0121) 622 5669

If you're quackers over crispy duck, nuts for satay pork, or could easily shovel down one ton of won ton, then the staggering menu at Chung Ying will make you weak at the Canton-knees. There are over 350 dishes to choose from, including a mighty selection of vegetarian fare, and if you do your (dim) sums, you'll find the prices are very reasonable to boot. Established back in the shoulder-padded days of 1981, Chung Ying is the 'original' name in Brum's China Town.

☻ *Mon–Sat, 12pm–11.30pm; Sun, 12pm–10.30pm*
🍴 *Beef with green peppers in*
black bean sauce, £7.80
🍷 *£10.50*

Eat

Del Villaggio

245 Broad Street

(0121) 643 4224

Real Italian food served by real Italians on the very un-Italian Broad Street. Almost every bar on the strip belongs to a chain, but Del Villaggio keeps its chain restaurant status quiet. A set menu and pleasing prices accompany interesting and fresh food that they'll happily personalise just for you. The head chef personifies Italian charm, working the tables like a pro and checking every last customer is happy. Best restaurant on Broad Street.

🕑 *Sun–Thu, 5.30pm–11pm;*
Fri–Sat, 5.30pm–11.30pm
🍴 *Monkfish with fresh seafood in chef's own chowder, £16.95*
💷 *£15.75*

Handmade Burger Co

Brindley Place

(0121) 665 6542

Chunky chips, forty different types of burger and you leave with change from a tenner. What's not to love? Well, rising obesity levels we guess, otherwise we can't think of a bad thing about this place. 'Take a seat, order at the counter' is the slogan, adding to the American diner feel created by the booths and sofas. Sadly, the waitresses don't scoot around on roller skates, but they are all young and friendly, making Handmade Burger Co a pleasing place to get your protein.

🕑 *Sun–Thu, 12pm–10.30pm;*
Fri–Sat, 12pm–11pm
🍴 *Tikka masala burger, £6.95*
💷 *£10*

Duet

Fort Dunlop, Erdington

(0121) 748 1234

Duet's concept might have seemed like a good idea at the time, but then so did the Millennium Dome. Did anyone actually ask for it in the first place? Duet caters to the terminally indecisive by offering both Indian and Italian dishes and, although they boast world-renowned chefs, the menu just leaves you confused. Do you have the same for every course or mix it up? The walls are bare and the music dire, giving it all the atmosphere of a service station. Big portions and decent prices don't mean much when less would be more.

🕑 *Mon–Sun, 12pm–11.30pm*
🍴 *Linguini al Duet, £11.95*
💷 *£9.99*

Jyoti

569–571 Stratford Road, Sparkhill

(0121) 766 7199

Jyoti's owner seems to have converted his front room into a bakery and whacked a restaurant on the side. With the glittering lights of their Indian sweet shop, the eatery is quite hard to spot. They serve up tasty homemade grub, completely animal-free, being the only veggie restaurant on Birmingham's curry mile. Oh, but you do have Jamie Oliver watching you as he once visited and every generation of every family in Sparkhill wanted a photo with him.

🕑 *Tue–Wed, 6pm–9.30pm; Thu–Sun, 1pm–3pm & 6pm–9.30pm; last orders strictly 9.15pm*
🍴 *Jyoti special masala dhosa, £5.95*
💷 *BYO*

Kinnarree

22 Waterfront Walk

(0121) 665 6568

With a candlelit longboat and umpteen Buddha statues as decoration, Kinnaree could pass as a Thai temple. Add to that the three pages of the menu dedicated to Thai food and culture and all images of Thailand as a land of ladyboys, cheap brides and tuk-tuks go out the window. Practically any Thai dish you can think of is on the menu and all of it's as authentic as the dress the staff shuffle around in. Tuk-tucked away behind the Mailbox, Kinnaree's location is the only thing that lets it down.

☺ *Mon–Fri, 12pm–3pm & 6pm–11pm; Sat, 12pm–11pm; Sun, 12pm–10.30pm*

🍴 *Flaming weeping tiger, £10.50*

💰 *£10.95*

The Loft Lounge

143 Bromsgrove Street

(0121) 622 2444

The Loft Lounge is Itchy's fave for a stylish feed-up. Winners of the 'Best Food' category in the 2007 Brum Bar and Club awards (as voted for by real live Brummies and their tummies), their cosmopolitan, freshly prepared menu spans everything from juicy burgers to venison and duck. They serve brunch all day too and offer 10% off everything on weekdays with their City Living discount scheme. The sumptuous surroundings are delicious to boot, with a suspended fireplace, exposed brickwork and swanky patio garden. True decadence.

☺ *Sun–Thu, 11am–11pm; Fri–Sat, 11am–11pm*

🍴 *Loft Lounge salad, £5.95*

💰 *£12.50*

Las Iguanas

Arcadian Centre,

Hurst Street

(0121) 622 4466

If you can resist the urge to shake that boo-tay to the mariachi long enough to eat, give yourself a pat on the back. In fact, maybe you should reward yourself with one of their fabulous caipirinha cocktails to wash down all the fine South American cuisine you've just scoffed. Two-for-one nights promise double the trouble. The lively and infectious atmosphere is perfect for big parties and the staff fall over themselves to make sure this won't be your last visit. Eat 'til you Ig-gy Pop.

☺ *Mon–Sun, 12pm–11pm*

🍴 *Sea bass, £13.50*

💰 *£12.50*

Eat

The Living Room
Unit 4 Regency Wharf 2, Broad Street
(0870) 442 2539

White leather sofas and soft jazz set the tone in this swish restaurant/bar. Don't let the address put you off – taking the lift up from Broad Street is like ascending to Prada from Primark. The long drapes and pot plants would be perfect for hiding behind, and it all feels a bit as if you might have stepped onto a James Bond set. For classic Connery devotees there's pies and bangers 'n' mash, and for those who didn't think Brosnan was half bad, go for the more modern roast organic salmon.

🕒 *Mon–Tue, 11am–1am; Wed–Sat,*
11am–2am; Sun, 11am–12am
🍴 *Seafood and saffron risotto, £10.95*
💷 *£14*

Milano
Ladywell Walk, Arcadian
(0121) 622 3999

If it's swanky sophistication you're after but without the bank-breaking price tag, Milano fits the bill. With glistening chandeliers and an impressive mirrored bar you'll feel like royalty, but still relaxed enough to put your elbows on the table. The pre-theatre set menu (two courses for £14.95) sets you up for an evening at the Hippodrome, and if you have room for dessert then hit yourself up with THE BEST profiteroles in the whole wide world. Capitals fully justified.

🕒 *Mon–Thu, 12pm–2.30pm & 5pm–*
10.30pm; Fri–Sat, 12pm–2pm & 5pm–11pm;
Sun, 4.30pm–10.30pm
🍴 *Lamb with chocolate sauce, £16.95*
💷 *£13.95*

Locanta
31 Ludgate Hill, St Pauls Square
(0121) 236 7227

Don't let the local chavs bawling obscenities across the road fool you; Locanta is situated in one of Birmingham's classier districts. Just make sure you are not one of those 'I speak with my hands' people because it can prove quite a struggle to keep the flowers, wine and food upright on a table for two that has the surface area of a frozen pea. Luckily the delicious food totally makes up for hand-waving hazards. If you like to roll out of a restaurant with your jeans bursting at the seams then Locanta is La Place for you.

🕒 *Mon–Sun, 12pm–12am*
🍴 *Seabass, £8.95*
💷 *£11.50*

Nando's
Bullring
(0121) 632 6866

Cheap chicken galore. Nando's offers girls with cheapskate boyfriends the chance of being taken to dinner. Hand over a tenner and you get plenty of change. But that's not all – mediocre grub, rude staff and a weight loss program where you starve to death before getting seated are also thrown in. Among a herd of hungry Brummies and 2.4-families, it's easy to hear a pin drop. If it dropped in your eye, that is. Not for those who like anything other than chicken.

🕒 *Mon–Thu, 12pm–10.30pm; Fri–Sat,*
12pm–11pm; Sun, 12pm–8.30pm
🍴 *1/4 chicken with chips and*
spicy rice, £5.50
💷 *£10.95*

Nathaniel's

13 St Mary's Row, Moseley

(0121) 449 9618

Simply one of the best bars in the city. The soft jazz blends perfectly with the simple black and white décor. Inventive, perfectly cooked and beautifully presented food add up to exactly what you want from a nice meal out, and what's more it's worth every penny. Attentive service, but not over-friendly. There if you need them but they'll leave you alone too. Like the food, the staff are just perfect. All the proof you need that very good things come in small packages.

☺ *Mon–Thu, 6.30pm–10pm; Sun, 12.30pm–3pm; Fri–Sun, 6.30pm–10.30pm*

🍴 *Pan-fried monkfish with chorizo, £11.95*

💰 *£13*

The Oriental

The Mailbox

(0121) 633 9988

The Oriental should be on your visit list if you like to be seen in the right places with the right faces. Specifically, faces of random Chinese folk which have been used as upholstery on the chairs – just one of the kitschy design features that make The Oriental feel quite cool. The food looks as good as the décor, but it would be a terrible waste to stick it in a picture frame on the walls. With Malaysian, Thai and Chinese making up the menu, it's like all your favourite takeaways rolled into one giant spring roll.

☺ *Mon–Fri, 5pm–11pm*

🍴 *Deep fried duck in plum sauce, £9.25*

💰 *£10.95*

Opus

54 Cornwall Street

(0121) 200 2323

No, you haven't got the wrong address, this isn't the Museum of Minimalism, though the bare walls and table settings could all be exhibits. But when it comes to what matters, they're far from stingy. Great food with long names is the name of the Opus game. But beware, once you've mastered the main course, the work-of-art desserts come and hit you like a custard to the face. There's absolutely no escaping them, we're afraid.

☺ *Sun–Fri, 12pm–2.30pm; Mon, 6pm–10pm; Tue–Fri, 6pm–10.30pm; Sat, 7pm–10.30pm;*

🍴 *Fillet of cod rarebit, regati pasta, spring greens and white wine cream sauce, £15.50*

💰 *£12.95*

Pennyblacks

132–134 Wharfside Street, The Mailbox

(0121) 632 1460

What's the best restaurant for a relaxed mid-week meal out with good food and a fine wine list? You said: Pennyblacks. Our survey said: PING! And where's the best place to go for good group grub? You said: Pennyblacks. Our survey said: PING! Then we asked you where they would go for a big, special night out. You said: anywhere but Pennyblacks. Our survey said: PING! Your prize? A meal at Pennyblacks, though of course, you're paying.

☺ *Mon–Thu, 10am–11pm; Fri–Sat, 10am–12am; Sun, 10am–10.30pm; food, Mon–Sat, 10am–10.30pm; Sun, 10am–9.30pm*

🍴 *Crab salad, £7.95*

💰 *£10.50*

Eat

Peppers

5b Bishopsgate Street

(0121) 633 4411

With a huge mural covering the domed roof, Peppers is a strong candidate for best ceiling in Brum. But looks aren't everything, so they've got a sexy menu to match. Indian, Thai and Chinese dishes mean there's lots of choice but spiciness is a dead cert. The toilets are also a sight to behold, with rubber sinks and metal buckets for urinals. There's also a machine dispensing disposable toothbrushes, probably after complaints that the curry was something of a repellent in the nearby clubs.

🕒 *Mon–Thu, 12pm–2.30pm & 6pm–11pm;*
Fri–Sat, 6pm–11.30pm; Sun, 2pm–10pm
🍴 *Lamb shank Massaman, £11.95*
💷 *£10.95*

Rooty Frooty

Custard Factory, Gibb Street, Digbeth

(0121) 224 8458

As the name suggests, Rooty Frooty is hip, healthy and very veggie. There's not a leg, breast or sliver of meat within a mile of the menu. Mostly vegan with four or five choices for lunch, and different sizes for different appetites. They've kitted it out with second hand furniture which gives it a bohemian, rather than tatty, feel. Lunch is popular with Custard Factory inhabitants so get there early to get the most choice. They don't stop at food though, bands and DJs play on some nights, with organic cider to fill your environmentally-friendly gut...

🕒 *Opening times vary*
🍴 *Three bean chilli, £4*
💷 *£10*

Red Peppers

The Mailbox

(0121) 643 4202

Like a sugar-coated bitter pill. Or a gift-wrapped poo. Or anything else crap but deceptively packaged. A beautiful restaurant, with leather seats, scented tea lights, excellent service and reasonable prices. Scrumptious starters aside, the menu boasts some of the worst food in Brum. Unless you enjoy semi-raw meat and vinegar-drowned salad, that is. Sit there and admire the surroundings, though, and you're in for a good night.

🕒 *Sun–Thu, 12pm–11.30pm;*
Fri–Sat, 12pm–12am
🍴 *Bruschetta topped with mushrooms and gorgonzola cheese, £4.95*
💷 *£12.50*

San Carlo

4 Temple Street

(0121) 633 0251

Seeing as they've put a lot of time into their décor, it's only fair that we give it the Itchy once over. Here goes: there's lots of blue glass, chrome and erm, baskets of fresh fruit and veg. Presumably they're trying to demonstrate the freshness of their ingredients. Sadly, with a pasta-heavy menu, the veg content's light enough for us to want to suggest Trading Standards come down on them like a ton of spuds. Still, wherever they get their ingredients, the excellent food and desserts justify the bill. Be warned though, service can be slow.

🕒 *Mon–Sun, 12pm–11pm*
🍴 *Seafood linguini in tomato sauce, £9.20*
💷 *£12.95*

Eat

Sanctum

110 Colmore Row

(0121) 236 1110

If Sanctum did takeaway, they'd be on to something. That way, you could just eat in your cellar at home instead of paying for the privilege of visiting theirs. Even better, you wouldn't have to spend five precious minutes of your life explaining what a glass of water is to the waitresses. Don't bother reading the menu, as it doesn't come close to describing what ends up on your plate. Bar One Ten upstairs is very pleasant. They just missed the 'Quit while you're ahead' chapter of the business manual.

🕒 *Mon–Fri, 12pm–3pm & 6pm–11pm; Sat, 6pm–11pm*

🍴 *Fillet of beef and pepper sauce, £16*

💷 *£12.50*

Sundarbon

590–592 Bristol Road, Selly Oak

(0121) 472 7858

There's five curry houses within a stone's throw of each other in studenty Selly Oak, but this one takes the bhuna. Free onion bhajis and an exquisite selection of dips to go with your poppadom swings it for them. No problem if you don't like your curry eye-wateringly spicy, as there's plenty for korma fans. Every dish on the menu seems to come highly recommended by someone; the chef, the restaurant, the manager or your gran. Good food, good prices, good times.

🕒 *Mon, Tue, Thu & Sun, 5pm–1.30am; Wed & Fri–Sat, 5pm–2.30am*

🍴 *Chicken tikka massala, £6.75*

💷 *£8.75 or BYO*

Simla

18 Boldmere Road

(0121) 354 1122

Boldmere in Sutton Coldfield is fast becoming a Balti belt, with more Indian restaurants on its quarter-mile strip than an equivalent street in Mumbai. Itchy's pick of the bunch is the newly opened Simla. Sadly they've moved away from the traditional flock-wallpaper décor and incongruous pan pipe melodies, and into the 21st century, with minimalist furniture and Bollywood on plasmas. Don't let that fool you, however, as the vast selection of traditional and fusion foods is as good as it is cheap. Also, to the delight of lager swillers, it's BYO.

🕒 *Mon–Sun, 5pm–12am*

🍴 *Jaipuri Madras, £7.95*

Tin Tin

9F Water's Edge, Brindleyplace

(0121) 633 0888

As far as we know, Tin Tin has no link to the Belgian boy detective. This small disappointment aside, this is the perfect Chinese restaurant for big gatherings. The huge menu, complete with the usual comedy misspellings, is full of dishes to share, and the staff are happy to dispense advice if you're a newbie. This is westernised Chinese food though – Tintin's canine companion Snowy is off the menu.

🕒 *Mon–Sun, 12pm–2.30pm (last orders 2.10pm) & 5.30pm–11.40pm (last orders, 11.10pm); Sat–Sun, 5.30pm–11pm (last orders, 10.40pm)*

🍴 *Crispy aromatic duck, £8.50*

💷 *£10.90*

Drink

Drink

Welcome to Drink

To be honest, when it comes to boozers, Brum has some real dives. Luckily for you, us lovely Itchy folk have done all the hard work for you and reviewed the best and the worst, so your evening's drinking need not be disturbed by sub-standard head. Which brings us nicely on to another of life's great pleasures: happy hour. It never seems to end at the **Figure of Eight (236-239 Broad Street, 0121 633 0917)**, where promos run from opening (9am, no less) 'til the last stragglers have fallen out the door. For an after-work/play wind down, it's 2-4-1 on cocktails at **Island Cocktail Bar (14-16 Suffolk Street Queensway, 0121 632 5296)**. With daily specials, you can go back between 5pm and 7pm every day and never get bored. Finally, **Apres (Broadway Plaza, 0121 456 4141)** has five hours of drunken happiness a day, with vast pitchers of delicious boozy drinks on special offer.

Top five cocktails

Night Cappuccino at Loft Lounge
Chocolate, coffee, cream, cracking.

Bisonoska at Red Bar and Lounge – Try saying that after a few pints.

Strawberry Fields at Mechu
You're not John Lennon so don't break into song at the bar.

Honey Berry Sour at Island Bar
High scorer at the best cocktail bar in town.

Cherry Cola at Revolution
Sweet, sweet vodka.

Top five most notable toilets

The Square Peg – Don't even think about stepping foot in this cesspit. Holding it in will be the best thing you ever did.

The Adam and Eve – Going to the loo has never been so much fun.

The Old Crown – Old pub, new toilets, no more outhouse.

Bar Risa – Slutty girls discussing who they've pulled. Score.

Tainted Halo – The trance is only slightly deafening once the cubicle door's closed.

How to make your pint last all day

befriend the nearest person who looks like they might have full pockets. Drunk that one too? Tell someone you're about to become a parent. Necked that one as well? Well, there's no helping you then...

Play coin football – Fact: if you're not actually drinking, your drink lasts longer. Indulge in a nice game of coin footie instead. Place three coins in a triangle formation, then flick them forwards one by one, using the coin that's furthest back, sliding it between the other two. The target is the makeshift goal your opponent has made with his fingers

HARD UP, BUT LIKE NOTHING MORE THAN WHILING AWAY TIME IN A BOOZER? FEAR NOT. A TRIP TO THE PUB NEEDN'T BREAK THE BANK

Keep the pint cool – Get yourself one of those chemical ice-packs for injuries. After an hour or so, crack it open, and wrap it around your beverage. Hey presto: it's like you've just bought it.

Go minesweeping – Some people just don't understand the value of the last two sips. Wait 'til these wasteful types have left the pub, then nip over and finish their backwash. Take the glass to the bar afterwards, and the bar staff'll love you so much they'll let you carry on all day.

Create fake identities – Running perilously low on that pint? Quick, pretend it's your birthday and

Get a job there – Hey, we've given you four top tips already. What more do you want from us? If you can't make a pint last all day with these gems, you're going to have to ask the landlord for a job.

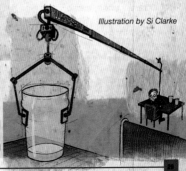

Illustration by Si Clarke

Drink

BARS

Apres Bar
Broadway Plaza, Five Ways
(0121) 456 4141

Apparently the log-burning fires and big sofas are in Apres to create a Scandinavian feel. No doubt plasma TVs have been in ski lodges for centuries, too. Technological impostors aside, they've done nicely on atmosphere, but their happy hours are the icing on the Scandie cake. From three 'til eight every day you can drink yourself silly on the cheap. You don't even have to leave for solid sustenance in between pitchers. During the week you and a friend can get pizza, salad and a bottle of wine for fifteen quid.

☻ *Sun–Thu, 10am–12am; Fri–Sat, 10am–1am*

Bennetts
8 Bennetts Hill
(0121) 643 9293

The columns at the entrance, high ceiling and stone floors positively scream 'I used to be a bank,' but the big, comfy seats and murals on the walls are welcome changes, and however nicely we ask, we've never managed to convince the staff to give us a tenner's worth of 20p pieces. It calls itself a wine bar, which does seem unnecessarily pompous, but does account for the suits and suits' secretaries that ram the place come lunchtime. On a busy night it can get quite jovial but don't come down here for a piss up or on the pull. Your boss could well be lurking in one of the many coves, and we all know how dangerous that can be.

☻ *Mon–Sat, 12pm–11pm; food, 12pm–9pm*

Bacchus
Burlington Arcade, New Street
(0121) 616 7991

Sweeping velvet drapes, secluded booths and dark panelled walls make Bacchus feel more like the Crystal Maze's medieval zone or the drawing room in Cluedo. You half wait for Richard O'Brien to swoop in and ask if you'll start with a physical or a mental challenge. The wealthy folk who grace the bar, though, are unlikely to know anything of such populist tomfoolery. The impressive interior and cosy feel make Bacchus unique, but the strictly over-21 door policy can be a touch problematic for studenty types.

☻ *Mon–Sat, 12pm–11pm; Sun, 12pm–10.30pm; food, Mon–Sat, 12pm–9.30pm; Sun, 12pm–6.30pm*

The Boiler Room
120 Vyse Street, Jewellery Quarter
(0121) 248 4999

The mixture of vintage furniture and modern, shiny bar sums up how eclectic the Boiler Room is. Live bands one night, then hip hop MCs the next, mean Forrest Gump's old dear was on the right track with her box of chocolates analogy – you never know what you're gonna get, but it's hard to care in a place this lovely. Jump in a cab, get away from the drunken idiots in the city centre and you won't regret it. Sofas and bean bags around the dance floor make a deceptively large venue feel cosy and intimate. Throw in a drinks list as inviting as the door staff and it's seriously hard to fault the place.

☻ *Opening times vary*

The Breakfast Club

186 Broad Street

(0121) 643 722

'Will you stand above me? Look my way, never love me? Rain keeps falling; rain keeps falling, down, down, down. Will you recognise me? Call my name or walk on by? Rain keeps falling; rain keeps falling down, down, down, down. Hey, hey, hey, hey. Ooohh... Don't you, forget about me. Don't, don't, don't, don't, don't, you forget about me...' Wait a minute, this place is nothing like *The Breakfast Club*. Where's Emilio? Where's Judd Nelson? Molly Ringwald certainly wouldn't be caught dead drinking the poncey cocktails and dancing to the incessant r 'n' b in here. Stay in and watch its namesake instead.

🕑 *Wed–Sun, 7pm–5am*

The Country Girl

1 Raddlebarn Road, Selly Oak

(0121) 414 9921

Blonde haired and buxom, The Country Girl slips you a sly wink as she leans over the bar to pour your pint. Oh dear, the pint seems to be overflowing. She teases the froth off the glass with her finger, licks it off, and brings it over to your seat. Oh, my, is it getting hot in here? Well yes, actually. Dotted with open fireplaces, The Country Girl boasts a warm and comforting atmosphere that those city girls with their silly white wine, white chocolate and the-whole of the-third-series-of-*Friends*-in one-night marathons can only dream of.

🕑 *Mon–Wed, 12pm–11pm; Thu,*
12pm–11.30pm; Fri–Sat, 12pm–12am;
Sun, 12pm–10.30pm

The Briar Rose

25 Bennetts Hill

(0121) 634 8100

The Briar Rose does everything a self-respecting Wetherspoons should do. It provides wallet-friendly post work or pre-club lubrication and a nice plate of cardboard cottage pie to line your stomach. This 'Spoons is considerably nicer than the Square Peg up the road, meaning the usual parade of career alcoholics tend to frequent the Peg, leaving the Rose free for office workers and the odd student. Apparently not a retirement home for ageing meteorologists, the Wetherlodge upstairs provides a cheap kip for you and your new best mate.

🕑 *Mon–Thu, 7am–12am; Fri, 7am–1am;*
Sat, 8am–1am; Sun, 8am–12am

The Factory Club

The Custard Factory, Gibb Street, Digbeth

(0121) 693 6333

Part of the Custard Factory, the only Birds you'll find here now are trendily clad and partying in the kind of style that would make Andy Warhol proud. This house of funk is known for its infectious atmosphere and outstanding live music. Hosting famous DJs and other live urban acts, the outdoor swimming pool is often drained and covered over with a marquee to accommodate the overflow. This should keep the queues for the drinks to a minimum. The fly in the custard is the toilets, which should be avoided if you can possibly bear to hold it. Otherwise, it's the diagnosis for any destination dilemma.

🕑 *Thu–Sat, 9pm–2am; club nights vary*

Drink

Glamourous

Albany House, 27–35 Hurst Street

(0121) 622 4770

So you're done up like it's opening night at *The Rocky Horror Picture Show*. Eyeliner? Check. *Hairspray*-styled beehive wig? Check. Electric blue sling-backs? Got 'em. You have the look, baby, and you're ready to sing along with the best of them, but where to go? Glamorous is the biggest and most fabulous blip on Birmingham's roving gaydar, and draws in the funloving crazy crowds, both gay and straight, for fun and frolics. Don't know the lyrics to Bonnie Tyler's power ballads by heart? Don't worry, we don't either, but you're still in for a fabulous time, daahling..

🕒 *Mon–Thu, 6pm–4am; Fri–Sun, 4pm–4am*

🎟 *Free entry*

Island Rock 'n' Roll Cocktail Bar

14–16 Suffolk Street, Queensway

(0121) 632 5296

Serious contenders for most convoluted name in the book. The only island it inhabits is one deserted of any other bars and surrounded by a dual carriageway. Rock 'n' Roll seems to be trying to drown out the whizzing traffic with songs from the Britpop era, while pictures of those that sang them replace the need for any wallpaper. But they have fulfilled their Cocktail Bar moniker with bottles being flung about like Frisbees. Slightly try-hard décor aside, Island's got a relaxed vibe, which means that it's not just another pretentious cocktail bar.

🕒 *Mon–Thu, 5pm–12pm; Fri–Sat, 5pm–2am*

Mechu

59 Summer Row

(0121) 212 1661

Mechu? Bless you. Itchy has to confess that this one had us poring over our thesaurus, wondering how many synonyms we could find for pretentious, over-rated, expensive or pseudo-classy. Notorious for its door policy, this review only made it into the guides in time because we were waiting so long to get past the bouncers that we got most of it written in the queue. There's nothing quite like 20 minutes stood listening to cheesy pop surrounded by twats in their uniform of slacks and slip-on loafers to get those creative juices flowing. On the plus side, despite the prices inside, it's not too expensive to get in.

🕒 *Mon–Sun, 11am–1am*

The Loft Lounge

143 Bromsgrove Street

(0121) 622 2444

This gorgeous, award-winning bar is an Itchy favourite. With new, swish signature cocktails, including Beverly Hills Iced Teas and different flavoured Daiquiris, plenty of speciality beers, and friendly, well-trained staff who get extra points for speed – we've never had too much time to kill-a waiting for tequila. Whether you fancy slumping back on a slouchy sofa at one of the low tables with a coffee to cure your hangover, or creating a new headache from scratch with Belgian beers and a boogie, you'll soon be holding this place a-Loft as one of Brum's best.

🕒 *Sun–Thu, 11am–12am; Fri–Sat, 11am–2am*

💰 *£12.50*

The Newt

58 Stephenson Place

(0121) 643 2969

If you've got half an hour to kill while you're waiting for your train, The Newt is conveniently located just below New Street station. Go back on yourself when you've come down the ramp from the Pallasades and you can't miss it. You wouldn't want it as your local, but there's a good chance of a space to park up, and a pint to please yourself. Being able to hear yourself think isn't a guarantee if it's a Saturday afternoon, but at least that might deter the nutter at the bar who think he's Jesus. And besides, who wants to hear themselves think anyway?

🕒 *Mon–Fri, 10am–12pm; Sat, 9am–2am; Sun, 12pm–8pm*

Oh Velvet

200 Broad Street

(0121) 248 0500

They say that at the end of the rainbow, a leprechaun hides a pot of gold. Well, however rainbow-like the lights of Broad Street, there's little golden (or indeed, Irish) in this pot. Cosmopolitans, Long Island Iced Teas and White Russians are the flavours of the day, so it's small wonder that the Guinness isn't served with crushed ice and a twist of lemon. Otherwise, vodka and Cranberries (geddit? geddit?) is about as Irish as it gets really, and you'd be just as well off at the local Walkabout for that authentic Irish feel. See, Enya glad you have a copy of Itchy? Yeah, that means U2.

🕒 *Mon–Fri, 12pm–2am; Sat–Sun, 12pm–3am*

Drink

The Old Contemptibles

176 Edmund Street

(0121) 200 3831

Forget your trendy wine bars and gastropubs, this is a public house of the traditional kind. They've got real ale, a small forest's worth of dark wood, a pair of slippers and even a pipe if you ask nicely. Recent refurbishments went easy on the metallic chrome, so the pub kept its old time charm but your pint no longer sticks to a grimy old table. Named after a group of World War One soldiers who used to meet here, there's history coming out of the woodwork, so you might actually learn something from that rambling loon in the corner. Something useful that is, not just how to frighten toddlers.

Ⓒ *Mon–Sat, 12pm–11pm*

The Patrick Kavanagh

142 Trafalgar Road, Moseley

(0121) 449 2598

If you want to gel with the Moseley locals, a good start is to drink here and call it by its proper name – the PK. You'll find it right on the corner of Trafalgar and Woodbridge Roads, and the bright purple exterior is a handy pointer. Although technically an Irish pub they avoid associations with tacky themed bars by harping on about the local vicar they were named after. With live comedy, music and footie, it's unlikely you'll get bored, while Itchy was recently told the PK is also 'the best place in Moseley to pull hotties', meaning the drinks are cheap enough to fit you out with beer goggles.

Ⓒ *Mon–Sat, 11am–11pm;*
Sun, 12pm–10.30pm

Old Joint Stock

4 Temple Row West

(0121) 200 1892

One of the swankier joints to be found in the city centre, the Old Joint Stock is the playground of Birmingham's burgeoning social elite and their hangers-on. The grandiose, columned entrance leads through to a swish island bar that might resemble your rich great aunt's jewellery box, if you have a rich great aunt. The large marble busts bedecking the walls are strangely paralleled by the heaving, silicon falsies of the nouveau-riche. A sight indeed. There's also a theatre though, and a pretty good sweep of beers and ales at hand, if the busts prove to be off limits.

Ⓒ *Mon–Sat, 11am–11pm; Sun, 12pm–*
10.30pm; food, Mon–Sun, 12pm–9pm

Poppy Red

Arcadian Centre, Hurst Street

(0121) 687 1200

Given that you can't really move in the Arcadian for plumbers and plasterers with the leftover cash from getting their hair sculpted to look like Timmy Mallet's cockatoo Magic wedged into the pockets of their tight white jeans, Poppy Red is a sanctuary of sorts. We emphasise, of sorts. Posing and preening, much like a cockatoo in fact, are still the reason most are here but the music's a bit more off-centre and there's room to dance or alternatively, sit in a corner and plot what you could throw to land right on top of Magic.

Ⓒ *Mon–Tue, 12pm–11pm; Wed–Sat,*
12pm–2am; Sun, 12pm–10.30pm

Drink

Red Bar and Lounge
Temple Street
(0121) 643 0194

Don't be put off by the dingy staircase leading up to Red, as your reward is sexy leather sofas and a very James Bond-style setting. Not everyone in here has 007's ego on them but there might be a few who earn more in a day than we do in a month/year/lifetime. The circle of admirers around such big hitters should be a clue, as half of them have faces like a punctured lung. For the rest of us plebs, Red's location in the business district makes it an excellent choice for an after-work drinking session. DJs and live acts get it going at the weekend.
🕒 *Mon–Tue, 12pm–8pm; Wed–Thu, 12pm–12am; Fri–Sat, 12pm–2am*

Rococo Lounge
260 Broad Street
(0121) 633 4260

Rococo suffers from a case of mistaken identity. On the surface you'd think it was a trendy lounge bar for quiet drinks, complete with a faintly pretentious booze list and candles adorning the tables in the seating area. The clientele, however are rather at odds with this, acting in fact as though a quiet drink is the last thing on their minds. They spend the night cheering for yet another funky house hit and getting far too pissed to know where the dance floor ends and the overcrowded sofa where Itchy is being rapidly crushed into a patch of seat the size of a postage stamp begins.
🕒 *Mon–Sat, 12pm–2am; Sun, 12pm–12.30am; food, 12pm–9pm daily*

Revolution
Unit 7 Five Ways, Broad Street
(0121) 665 6508

Like your vodka? Then look no further. Apparently there are one hundred different ways to drink vodka. No, we aren't sure what they all are either but when it comes to alcohol we're always open to suggestions? This is a great pre-club bar but due to its late licence you may find yourself so battered that you forget to move on. With the surroundings to attract business types and prices to attract students this place has got the balance of chic and cheerful just right.
🕒 *Mon–Sun, 11.30am–2am; food, Mon–Sun, 12pm–8pm*
🍴 *Steak flatbread, £5.95*
💷 £10
🎟 Free–£2

Slug and Lettuce
The Waters Edge, Brindley Place
(0121) 633 3049

An evening spent at the Slug and Lettuce is something like that scene in *Terminator II* where Sarah Connor imagines a playground being laid to waste in a fiery explosion. It's messy, scary, and you're not sure why it's happening to begin with. One might think that, like its eponymous mollusc, the Slug and Lettuce would endorse a vegetarian ethic, but not so much. Having said that, if they just served lettuce, you'd probably feel slightly hard done by. You're not going to win awards for originality by coming here, but at least you get more than just salad.
🕒 *Mon–Wed, 9am–11pm; Thu, 9am–12am Fri, 9am–1am; Sat, 10am–1am; Sun, 10am–10.30pm*

Drink

The Square Peg

115 Corporation Street

(0121) 236 6530

Are you a bulbous-nosed, ruddy-faced type whose daily routine involves an 11am dig around your pockets to collect enough change for a cheapo pint of watered-down ale? Then it's the Square Peg for you, old fella. Grab your copy of the *Racing Post*, and head on over to join like-minded wrinklies muttering at thin air, propped up against what was apparently once Europe's longest bar, but which is now just Birmingham's. The cheap food and booze prices mean it gets rammed come office closing and lunchtime too, so you'll have to be quick off the mark to get a seat.

☻ *Sun–Thu, 10am–11pm; Fri–Sat, 10am–12am*

Tarnished Halo

21 Ludgate Hill, Jewellery Quarter

(0121) 236 7562

The Tarnished Halo deserves an award. Never have we known a bar to do everything so spectacularly badly. While free, and generally empty during the week, on Saturday nights they install a trance DJ who assumes the crowd is hard of hearing. Should you forget to pay at the door, one of the friendly and welcoming bouncers will manhandle you back to the entrance and demand his three quid. At this point, don't make our mistake. Refuse to pay, turn around and get the hell out of there. Note: we have not exaggerated for comedic value. It's really that bad. Less Tarnished Halo, more poo-covered devil's fork.

☻ *Mon–Fri, 12pm–11pm; Sat, 12pm–late*

The Sunflower Lounge

76 Smallbrook Queensway

(0121) 632 6756

Great for retro tunes and live bands, near the station but away from Broad Street's lager louts. Beer-guzzling bozos come here too but their jeans are tighter, their hair's quiffed, not quaffed, and they resemble Johnny Rotten instead of Vegas. Comfy sofas greet you on arrival, but mild concussion waits downstairs. If you're going out for a 'good ol' catch-up' though, it won't happen here, unless you carry a megaphone.

☻ *Mon–Tue, 12pm–11.30pm; Wed–Thu, 12pm–1am; Fri, 12pm–1.30am; Sat, 12pm–2am; Sun, 5pm–11.30pm; food, 4pm–9pm*

⑪ *Broccoli pasta, £5*

☻ *£8*

The Trocadero

17 Temple Street

(0121) 616 2631

The Trocadero's clientele are the sort who like a quick pint of cold Carling and their food ordered from a sticky, laminate menu. This can be traced to the genius of its location just off New Street and a short stagger from the train station. You wouldn't know The Troc was once a grandiose Victorian fire station, at least not from the types who light it up these days. Look out for the pub's resident bearded, be-suited, carpet-bag-carrying loon, an Uncle Albert-esque raconteur who'll regale you with whatever's on his mind for the bargain price of a half of mild.

☻ *Sun–Thu, 11am–11pm; Fri–Sat, 11am–12pm; food, Mon–Sun, 12pm–8pm*

Walkabout

266–271 Broad Street

(0121) 632 5712

If being Australian means bars that try as hard as this yet fail as badly, then Rolf Harris can stick his kangaroo where the sun don't shine. Bright yellow paint must've been going cheap down B&Q 'cos we can't think of any reason why you'd drench every surface, wall and bog door with it otherwise. The front door's tended by aching-to-be-Aussie bouncers who exclude anyone who isn't wearing bright yellow. Maybe. This place doesn't deserve witty rhetoric. Two words suffice: stay away.

🕒 *Tue–Sat, 12pm–3am;*
Sun–Mon, 12pm–2am

🍴 *Burgers from £7.25*

💰 *£7.95*

The Yardbird

Paradise Place

(0121) 212 2524

The Yardbird, Birmingham's sexiest live music joint, is as close as you can get to 1920s New Orleans without stepping into a black and white detective flick. Believe us, kid – when we say that these jazz rhythms are the cat's meow, we know our onions. The cosy, low-lit bar provides plenty of opportunity for beating yer gums over some classy broad across the bar, or tapping the night away under the sway of that funky muzak. Winehouse and Brand clones have adopted it as home, but who cares if it looks like Edward Scissorhands did their hair when the beats are this slick?

🕒 *Wed, Sun, 11am–12am;*
Thu–Sat, 11am–2am

Drink

PUBS

The Actress and Bishop
36 Ludgate Hill
(0121) 236 7426

By day the Actress is full of suits on their lunch break, here for the pub grub, a pint of real ale and a pew in the big seating area. By night, especially at the weekend, local bands take over the upstairs gig room and bring with them a young, or young at heart, indie/rock crowd. All are 'Well into the local scene, man', almost as much as they're well into their lager. Everyone's very friendly, so get in there and throw yourself about a bit. As the actress said to the bishop.

⊙ *Sun–Fri, 12pm–2am; Sat, 5.30pm–2am;*
food, Mon–Sun, 12pm–3pm

The Adam and Eve
201 Bradford Street, Digbeth
(0121) 693 1500

Ever so slightly hidden in the depths of industrial Digbeth, this little beauty is a haven for music lovers with its impressive weekly schedule of live bands. Quality can vary but with a place this friendly, it's hard to care. A small but comfortable pub with a cracking pool room and a bunch of regulars straight out of *Cheers*. They all pack in for happy hour, Monday to Friday, 4pm–7.30pm and late licensing from Thursday to Saturday. We suggest you join them, and indulge in an appropriately-named pint of snakebite.

⊙ *Mon–Wed, 11am–11pm; Thu–Sat,*
11am–2am; Sun, 12pm–12.30am;
food, Mon–Fri, 12pm–2pm

Bristol Pear
679 Bristol Road, Selly Oak
(0121) 414 9981

Nestled in the heaving bosom of Selly Oak's studentville is a pair (or more accurately a pear, but there we go) that will make your mouth water. Decently sized and pert, the Bristol Pear offers pleasantly cheap pints and does a pretty mean burger too. While always popular with the local, studenty clientele, you can still normally find a place to nestle in there, and despite being a fairly big pear, this joint has the cosy, comforting atmosphere of your local boozer. Next time you want to get off your tits, get on down there. One of the breast bars in the area, you'd be knockers to miss out.

⊙ *Mon–Sat, 11am–11pm;*
Sun, 12pm–10.30pm

The Bull's Head

23 St Mary's Row, Moseley
(0121) 449 0586

The Bull's Head is to Moseley what Chesney Hawkes is to student unions. It has nearing mythical status and will keep coming back in one form or another for as long as its fans continue to clamour for it. Comfy leather sofas and lighting that's possibly too cool for its own good make up the interior, though you'll be grateful for half light and a few nice, loud tunes when the third weirdo in a row slides up to you at the bar. Drunks aside, there's an eclectic mix of Moseley locals propping up the bar. It's not too expensive a job either, and perfect for a chilled Sunday afternoon down t' pub.

🕐 Sun–Thu, 12pm–11.30pm;
Fri–Sat, 12pm–2am

Elizabeth of York

12a St Mary's Road
(0121) 442 5250

The Elizabeth of York is neither refined nor regal, being daughter to one JD Wetherspoon. She's more of a good time girl of a pub: cheap, outgoing and hanging about on a corner. Like other good time girls, she is constantly in demand on her busy nights and service can be slow. But the atmosphere makes up for this with merry folk dropping in for a quickie. Like many a jaunty wench, Elizabeth has a long history and the writing on the wall provides you with many nuggets of local history and a bit about the old girl herself. God bless the old maid.

🕐 Mon–Sat, 10am–11pm;
Sun, 12pm–10.30pm

Craven Arms

47 Upper Gough Street
(0121) 632 6388

Snuggled just behind the Mailbox is a Victorian pub that packs a walloping pint. If your idea of 'Victorian' is one of those ankle length black skirts, stockings and lace trimmings and a cheeky wink, then this place will definitely tickle your fancy. Whether your poison is a pint of pale ale, a brandy and Coke, or six or seven snakebites, this place will deliver with gusto. The Craven Arms offers a cosy period atmosphere, but you just know that underneath all those skirts and petticoats, she ain't wearing any knickers.

🕐 Mon–Thu, 9am–11pm; Fri, 9am–2am;
Sat, 12pm–2am; Sun, 12pm–6pm;
breakfast, 9am–11am; Sun, 12pm–5pm

Flapper and Firkin

Kingston Row
(0121) 236 2421

One of those multi-generational gaffs, where grizzled old-timers rub shoulders with fresh-faced misfits. Their weekly quiz night always goes down like 2-for-1 at Primark, and down the stairs, bands play to eager crowds packed into a tiny room with a stage the size of your average car boot and about as much breathing space. Back upstairs there's pool tables and a pretty well-stocked bar with your standard lagers plus a couple of ales. Grub ain't bad either, with pub lunches aplenty.

🕐 Mon–Thu, 12pm–11pm; Fri–Sat,
12pm–12am; Sun, 12pm–10.30pm;
food, Mon–Sun, 12pm–3pm

🍴 £6.50

Drink

The Green Man

2 High Street

(0121) 427 0961

Big boozer on the corner of Harborne high street. The cosy and friendly atmosphere keeps the fact that they're part of a chain well-hidden. The menus aren't revolutionary but the real ales change when head office gives the nod. Popular with locals and some students, especially on quiz nights and Sundays when they do a good roast dinner (remember to get there early). The staff don't hide their boredom too well but the big bar means that, even at busy times, service isn't too slow. Nice for Sunday lunch but not top of the 'out on the razz' list.

Mon–Sat, 11am–11pm; Sun, 12pm–10.30pm; food, Mon–Sun, 12pm–8pm

The Hill

23 Bennetts Hill

(0121) 631 3548

With stiff competition from the 14 squillion other pubs within a one mile radius, it's hard to shine on Bennetts Hill. But with more thirsty workers rushing out of their offices come five o'clock than there are pints to fill 'em, everywhere's heaving of an evening. The Hill fits comfortably into the 'mediocre' bracket. It wouldn't be anyone's local, but equally it's not just local tramps who frequent it. Special offers keep the drink prices pleasantly pocket-palatable, and there's standard pub food to line your gut. If you can't make it any further up the hill, this pub is a perfectly good second choice.

Mon–Sat, 11am–11.30pm; Sun, 11am–10.30pm

The Gun Barrels

Bristol Road

(0121) 471 2672

Walking in to this pub during the day is dangerous. It's so dark inside that you need to stand still for five minutes while your eyes adjust, or risk stacking it down the stairs. Visual impediments aside, the large 'Gunnies', as it is lovingly referred to by its regulars, is one of the most popular student haunts in Birmingham. During the summer months the beer garden's stuffed to the fences and it's a firm favourite all year round. The range of cheap alcohol guarantees annihilation, allowing you to misbehave guilt-free and get you in the mood for a serious night out.

Mon–Sat, 11am–11pm; Sun, 12pm–10.30pm

The Market Tavern

210 Moseley Street, Digbeth

(0121) 622 5998

Orienteering skill is a must-have to find this incredibly cool old boozer, along with maybe a bivvy bag and Kendal mint cake, but don't let that put you off wandering down on a Sunday to experience a spot of performance poetry at their regular open mic event. Alternatively, join the funked up punks for one of the many sweaty gigs held upstairs. Complete with traditional dodgy pub carpets, you could do worse than soak up the atmosphere and a pint with the rosy-cheeked regulars. You feel like you've earned it as one of the lucky few who managed to track the damned place down.

Ⓔ *Mon–Sun, 12pm–11pm;*
food, Mon–Sun, 12pm–3pm

Jug of Ale

43 Alcester Road

(0121) 449 1082

If Michelin stars were awarded to pubs, the Jug (its contents were dropped from the Brummie patois years ago) would get three. A long-standing favourite with the Moseley crowd and always full to the brim with locals, young and not-so-young. No student nights here, this one is for students of that ancient seat of learning: the University of Life. Weeknights are themed – Wednesdays' cheap pints and bands make it one of the best places for live music. You can even take your non-music-y mates and leave them in front of the widescreen footy. There we go, now everyone's happy.

Ⓔ *Mon–Sat, 11am–11pm;*
Sun, 12pm–10.30pm

The Old Crown

188 High Street, Deritend

(0121) 248 1368

The 700-year history of the Crown could probably fill an Itchy guide twice over so don't even think about bringing it up with a regular. The distinctive black and white building looks like the creation of a Hollywood film set with beams aplenty and a front door not unlike that of a hobbit hole. Inside ain't bad either, with a cosy bar area and restaurant on the side, plus rooms to rent upstairs. As if that wasn't enough, there's a very handy beer/smoking garden out the back. The über-trendy Custard Factory next door pales in comparison to this beauty.

Ⓔ *Mon–Sun, 11am–11pm; food, Mon–Sat,*
12pm–3pm & 5pm–9pm; Sun, 1pm–5pm

Scruffy Murphys

Newton Street, Dale End

(0121) 236 2035

Publicising yourselves as 'Birmingham's premier rock pub' then choosing a name that brings to mind leprechauns and shamrocks shows some balls. But then so does dressing entirely in black all year round. Scruffy's may draw an alternative crowd, and the blacked out windows may look a little foreboding, but they're a friendly and welcoming bunch. Service is quick, drink is cheap(ish) and there are plenty of nooks and crannies to hide away in should the music get a little too loud. With the Academy two minutes away, it's also a prime venue for pre- or post-gig drinks.

Ⓔ *Mon–Thu, 11am–12am; Fri–Sat,*
12pm–3am; Sun, 12pm–12am

Drink

The Station

Station Street, Sutton Coldfield

(0121) 362 4961

The ever-popular Station can proudly call itself the best pub in Sutton Coldfield. This award is based on a very extensive and impartial survey conducted with the four men propping up the bar one rainy evening. We can't find many reasons to knock it though, so we're not arguing. They've got good beer, friendly staff, a wholesome menu and a lively calendar of events. Perhaps most importantly though, The Station possesses a sizeable and covered outdoor area for smoking lepers, shunned from the pub by those out to ruin their lung-destroying fun.

🕒 *Sun–Thu, 12pm–11pm; Fri–Sat, 12pm–12am*

The Three Horseshoes

1273 Pershore Road, Stirchley

(0121) 458 1378

Whether three horseshoes are meant to be luckier than one we're not sure, but with live footy on the big screen, karaoke on a Thursday and real ale to boot, this could be three pubs in one. Add to that a couple of pool tables and music by the Stirchley-renowned Ronnie Rocket and you've got yourself a good ol' time. The Rocket's fan-club piles in at the weekends when it becomes a bit of a meat market, with the oldies looking on. The pub grub isn't quite so stomach-churning.

🕒 *Mon–Wed, 11am–11pm; Thu, 11am–12am; Fri–Sat, 12pm–1am; Sun, 11am–12am; food, Mon–Sat, 11am–7pm; Sun, 12pm–7pm*

The Tap and Spile

10–15 Gas Street

(0121) 632 5062

Just by Birmingham's major clubbing hub, the Tap & Spile seems worlds away from raucous Broad Street. You're more likely to see a canal boat captain hacking up a greenie into a spittoon than a raver snorting gak off a toilet seat here. The Tap & Spile has a very laid-back and rustic charm, making it popular with a more refined local crowd. With its pretty canalside location and the regular live music acts that grace its floorboards, you're in for a pretty darn good evening. Apart from anything else it's also great for a pint of ale and a pub lunch too.

🕒 *Mon–Thu, 12pm–11pm; Fri–Sat, 12pm–1am; Sun, 12pm–10.30pm*

Waxy O'Connors

184 Broad Street

(0121) 632 6562

About as Irish as Michael Flatley, this place makes a trip to O' Neill's feel like a horseback holiday to the blarney stone. They must've hacked up a small forest to provide the reams of wood fittings, and the number of Irish flags covering every surface is surely single-handedly keeping a whole Emerald Isle village's economy going. If you're a polyester-mix tie-wearing businessmen staying at the Novotel over the road, join your corporate-trip ilk in supping Guinness and watching *River Dance* on repeat. If you possess a modicum of taste, however, stay away.

🕒 *Mon–Wed, 12pm–11pm; Thu–Sat, 12pm–2am; Sun, 12pm–10.30pm*

The Wellington

37 Bennetts Hill

(0121) 200 3115

Birmingham's biggest real ale venue is also home to Birmingham's biggest beer guts. A strict dress code is observed: 25 square foot of stonewashed denim and a T-shirt from a 60s beer festival. With fifteen or so ales on tap, The Wellington offers something for everyone from beer-beginners to the more seasoned ale drinker. So as not to distract from the beer, the Wellie doesn't serve food, but cutlery and plates are provided should you want to bring your own. Having been here since water was turned into wine, they've learnt that allowing the bingers to line their gut is in the carpet's interest.

🕒 *Mon–Sun, 10am–12am*

The Rainbow

160 Digbeth High Street

(0121) 772 8174

An open-air courtyard round the back sets The Rainbow apart from the ranks of other Digbeth pubs. Live bands and DJs come out to annoy the neighbours, with a barbeque wafting the sweet smell of charcoal their way too. The hospitable bar, meanwhile, is always packed with pre-drinkers taking a pit stop on the way to the nearby clubs. Live events feature a mix of urban and rock music so in the spirit of universalism, rappers debate beats and bleeps with trendy indie kids. Itchy's favourite pub for a sunny afternoon, or a hot night for that matter.

🕒 *Times vary; food, Mon–Sun, 12pm–7pm*

💰 *£2–£8*

Yard of Ale

New Street

(0121) 616 7901

Narrow, underground and formerly the Tavern in the Town until it was bombed by the IRA in 1974. Are we selling it you yet? No, it's probably sounding about as attractive as spending your summer holiday in Kabul. Lesson learned, tours of terrorist atrocities were never going to attract the crowds so the Yard of Ale was born. Inside it's a bit dingy and a bit grotty but it's traditional and cheap for central Birmingham. For those allergic to chrome and imported bottled lager, the Yard is one of a rapidly dwindling band of unaffected, honest pubs in the city centre.

🕒 *Mon–Sat, 12pm–11pm;*
Sun, 12pm–10.30pm

Dance

Right on Queue

DO YOU EVER FIND YOURSELF STANDING IN A LONG LINE TO ENTER A CLUB, GET A DRINK, OR GO FOR A PEE? THEN YOU'LL FIND ITCHY'S Q-TIPS ON WAYS TO AMUSE YOURSELF WHILE YOU HANG ABOUT WORTH THEIR WAIT IN GOLD

Get the party started before you even hit the floor. Just bring a bag of thick elastic bands to hand out to fellow queue-tey pies, and get everyone to pluck a different note. When you're at the bar, try blowing over the tops of bottles to entertain the other punters. If you're good enough, they might throw you enough loose change to pay for your drink.

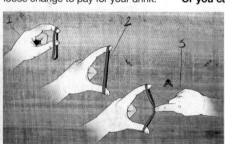

Before striding out, get down to the pound shop and buy a big bottle of the foulest perfume you can find, or even better, nip to a fishing shop and get your mitts on a bottle of lobster essence used for scenting baits. When waiting for a loo cubicle, pretend to be a toilet attendant, and offer exiting punters a free spritz of 'fragrance'. Every pongy person you zap with your minging musk is one fewer rival to compete against in the pulling stakes.

Or you can try the following trick. Start your evening at home by chowing down on beans and bhuna. Later, when you find yourself so far back in line that the folk at the front are in a different postcode, let the gas go. Watch the crowds shrink as they run from your stink, and try to figure out who it was who let rip. Don't strain too hard though, unless you fancy wandering home with the contents of your bowels sloshing around your smalls.

CLUBS

Air

Heath Mill Lane, Digbeth

(0845) 009 8888

If you refer to yourself as a 'cheesy quaver' that likes to 'ave it large' then seek out like-minded individuals at this Mecca of clubbing entertainment. The dance floors are connected by winding staircases that never seem to end up where you expect them to, making games of hide-and-seek a diverting option. Famous house and drum 'n' bass DJs frequently spin their LPs to produce pleasing beats that will make you shake them bones. Shame on you if you visit and don't end up pulling a sickie the next morning. You obviously weren't trying hard enough.

🕒 *Wed–Sun, 10pm–6am*

The Custard Factory

Gibb Street, Digbeth

(0121) 604 7777

The former Bird's factory is now a complex of art galleries, shops and studios by day and an outdoor club by night. It's not all dancing in the rain, the lake gets covered over to make a dance floor and makeshift dance tents fill up the courtyards. Our favourite bit is the stages they set up under the old railway arches, it's like an impromptu gig on an industrial estate. Line-ups are full of weird and wonderful performers so don't expect a night of club anthems. But you can usually bank on drum 'n' bass, dance and hip hop acts with some tribal drumming for the come down. The best night out in Brum.

🕒 *Times and prices vary*

Dragon Eye

193–194 Broad Street

(0121) 632 5113

Young, fashion-conscious, stick thin, high cheek-boned, image-obsessed individual seeks club with chic surroundings. Enjoys funky house and electro, which the DJ swears is fashionable in all the hottest clubs these days. Happy to join the queue of men at the bar trying desperately to attract members of the opposite sex, while avoiding the dance floor in case it messes with their perfectly sculpted hair. Real music enthusiasts, head anywhere else for a good time. There, you can wear what you like, rather than having to follow an implausible door policy.

🕒 *Thu, 10pm–2.30am; Sat, 10pm–2.30am*

💷 *Free–£5*

Dance

Flares

35 Broad Street

(0121) 632 5501

70s throwback club for those who think John Travolta's still got it. The *Saturday Night Fever* dance floor could be straight out of the film but the similarities stop at the drunk, middle-aged women who look like how Olivia Newton John might have turned out after a twenty year crystal meth habit. If you're at Flares against your will, always remember that standing at the bar cringeing won't get you out of there any faster. So borrow your dad's old flares and show you can rock around the clock with the best of them. If anything goes wrong, you can blame it on the boogie.

○ *Mon–Thu, 9pm–2am; Fri–Sat, 8pm–3am; Sun, 9pm–1am*

Oceana

Hurst Street

(0121) 632 6273

What Oceana should be is seven rooms with seven themes of music with seven globally-inspired names. What Oceana actually is is six empty rooms save the uninterested, asleep or bored bar staff and one amazing room, Icehouse Reykjavik. Have enough to drink, hit the dance floor and under the flashing lights, the all white décor feels a teeny bit like heaven. With a 1,000 person capacity and comfy sofas to rest tired feet, the ice house is a club of its own. As for the rest of Oceana, we can take it or leave it.

○ *Mon, 9pm–3am; Tue, 5pm–9pm; Wed–Thu, 9pm–3am; Fri–Sat, 8pm–3.30am*

€ *£3–£10*

The Jam House

3–5 St Paul's Square, Hockley

(0121) 200 3030

Jools Holland's bar in the Jewellery Quarter is hot stuff if you're a soul man or woman. We may be in the Midlands but judging from the queue round the block, that southern spirit's alive and kicking. Anything to the left of centre gets a place on the Jam House bill, with jazz, blues and funk taking centre stage. They pull in a classy crowd and they intend to keep it that way – you ain't getting in if you're under 21 or wearing the wrong rags. Maybe time to give that sophisticated look a whirl, eh?

○ *Tue–Wed, 6pm–12am; Thu, 6pm–1am; Fri–Sat, 6pm–2am*

€ *Tue–Wed, free; Thu, £5 after 9pm; Fri–Sat, £5 after 8pm, £8 after 10pm*

Q Club

212 Corporation Street

(0121) 212 1212

Logic would probably say that naming your club after the one activity that clubbers loathe most is about as sensible as calling your pub 'T Total'. Perhaps the name has its origins in the years of the Q Club's former glory. Itchy's far too fresh-faced to remember any of that but we hear that in its heyday this massive club was the site of some of the best raves in Brum. They're hoping to keep up the good work in the revamped building, originally built as a Methodist chapel. We'll say a little prayer for you when you're knelt at the toilet the next morning. Just because we're thoughtful like that.

○ *Thu–Sun, 10pm–6am*

The Sanctuary

78 Digbeth High Street

(0121) 633 8311

The Sanctuary is a Birmingham institution. Literally. Built to house the criminally insane, it evolved into a theatre before the five-storey Victorian building became the scene of more intense clubbing than at a seal colony. Whether it's indie kids with bad haircuts, gurning ravers or brrrrrapping hip hoppers, most Brummie 20-somethings will have a Sanctuary story to tell. And quite probably a long-lost coat swallowed up by the cloak room after paying a pound for the privilege. Barfly occupies the basement and hosts bands most nights of the week as well as club nights of wildly varying quality.

🕲 *Times and prices vary*

The Works

182 Broad Street

(0121) 633 1520

We once heard The Works described as 'the worst night out in Britain', and short of spending your Saturday night eating light bulbs, that's probably a fair description. Ladies and gents, welcome to hell. Factory-themed fittings dangle above hordes of degenerates standing in line for the bogs, funky house provides the soundtrack for the pending brawls, and stags and hens crowd the dancefloor desperate for any kind of penetration. It's best to avoid it, but if you're in Birmingham for any length of time, a visit becomes inevitable. Call it an initiation you'd rather not pass.

🕲 *Mon & Wed–Fri, 9.30pm–3am;*

Sat, 9.30pm–4am

Snobs

29 Paradise Circus, Queensway

(0121) 643 5551

Dark, dirty and cheap. Yes, the 'snob' label eludes us too, but it's not stopped Big Wednesdays becoming legendary. Many have tried to match it but it retains its title as the best alternative mid-week club night for chugging vodka of uncertain origin and swaggering to indie, sixties and northern soul tunes. Thursday nights are reserved for Sabotage (of the liver) to the racket of electro-trash and nu-rave. Brum's sleaze kings and queens rule the dance floor with the odd boozed-up emo type vying for strutting space.

🕲 *Wed, 9.30pm–3am; Thu, 10pm–2.30am;*

Fri–Sat, 10pm–3am

🕲 *£1.50–£5*

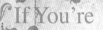

Gay

Gay

Drag Kings: A Very British Affair

MEN WHO DRESS AS WOMEN ARE OLD HAT. ITCHY'S MUCH MORE OF A FAN OF THE NATION'S NEWEST GAY CRAZE – WOMEN DRESSING AS MEN. MOVE OVER DRAG QUEENS: HERE COME DRAG KINGS

Following its brief moment in the spotlight during Victorian music hall performances, drag king shows – where women dress as men – may have pretty much vanished, but they're just about to make a comeback.

Some king performers take on realistic male personas on the stage by strapping down the chest area, 'packing' (typically created by sock-filled condoms), and adding realistic facial hair. Performances are usually mimed comic songs, performed as a 'troupe' of band members. However, solo performers, who take the act into wilder and more feisty territory, are becoming increasingly common.

Worldwide, 'kinging' has moved on from the days of old, but backward Britannia is still dragging her high heels. Drag queens have long been accepted in the gay scene, and more recently in mainstream entertainment, but sadly drag kings are yet to gain the same widespread popularity.

Illustration by Si Clarke

There is some hope though. The annual Transfabulous Festival is a big showcase for drag kings, and the Wotever World group hosts a variety of different drag king-packed nights. If this risqué revolution does take hold, we reckon there's no reason drag kings shouldn't have as much stage-space as their long-successful queen counterparts. Perhaps the art of female cross-dressing is about to come home...

BARS

Missing

48 Bromsgrove Street

(0121) 622 4256

A camp old cabaret bar run by camp old drag queens, filled with a camp old audience that's been around aeons longer than we thought campers had existed for. Tuesday night means Missing's own brand of bingo, and we all know nothing beats whacking out your marker, especially when it's free to play and comes complete with scathing insults from the two glamorous hostesses. Obviously we're using the term in its loosest sense, but we can't get enough, so don't let all our appalling innuendo put you off this charming show stopper.

☻ *Mon–Sun, 12pm–late*

The Pink Planet

148-151 Bromsgrove Street

No phone

No rose-tinted glasses required – the Pink Planet is Birmingham's most fabulous contemporary lesbian bar. With a grand opening serving up champagne and chocolate by the fountainful last year, Pink Planet promised to be something special. And it hasn't disappointed. Their live acoustic nights are great fun and with open mic and comedy nights on the cards, the Pink Planet is all set to tread pink pawprints all over Birmingham's gay scene. With its friendly atmosphere and great music policy, this lively bar will hand you a great time on a pink platter, served up with pink champagne and cherries on top.

☻ *Times vary*

The PINK PLANET

148-151 BROMSGROVE STREET B5 6RJ

Contemporary lesbian bar

Gay

PUBS

Equator

123 Hurst Street
(0121) 622 5077

Hurst Street's Equator is perhaps more tepid than tropical, but when it's just a quick one after work, frankly who cares? Hot beats and boys are few and far between in these tropics, but that's not the best that Equator has to offer. One of the more chilled out haunts in the gay village, put your feet up and unwind, or else grab your Itchy guide, and get on with planning that big night out. Equator makes a pretty good starting point, whether or not you choose to migrate south to more intense settings.

Ⓒ *Mon–Thu & Sun, 12pm–11pm;*
Fri–Sat, 12pm–12am

Glamourous Show Bar

Albany House, 27–35 Hurst Street
(0121) 622 4770

So you're done up like it's opening night at *The Rocky Horror Picture Show*. Eyeliner? Check. Hairspray-styled beehive wig? Check. Huge stilettos? Got 'em. You have the look, baby, and you're ready to sing along with the best of them, but where to go? Glamorous is the biggest and most fabulous blip on Birmingham's roving gaydar, and draws those fresh out the closet up to the most seasoned queens, jiggling their fanny packs in delight. Don't know the lyrics to Bonnie Tyler's power ballads by heart? Don't worry, we don't either, but you're still in for a fabulous time, daahling.

Ⓒ *Mon–Fri, 4pm–4am; Sun, 4pm–3am*

Subway City

27 Water Street
(0121) 233 0310

Subway City isn't a strictly gay club so whether you're into men, women or are undecided, you'll fit in here. The music's just as mixed up with seven rooms competing for the crowds with electro, urban, house, garage and shed, if you're lucky. Clubbers jump and prance like Tickle-Me Elmo, and if that sounds appealing, their monthly hard house all-nighter will be right up your street. For tamer souls, there's a café on the top floor where you can sit down and have a cuppa. If that sounds more your bag, then probably best avoid Subway.

Ⓒ *Thu, 10pm–4am; Fri, 10pm–6am;*
Sat, 10pm–8am
Ⓐ *Thu–Sat, £3–£10*

CLUBS

DV8

16 Kent Street/Lower Essex Street

(0121) 666 6366

A notorious club on the Brum scene, offering all-you-can-drink for as little as seven pounds. Sometimes the vodka tastes like it might as well be bleach, but by that point you're already too busy gyrating like a fat dog on the sticky wooden floor to care. Beware of emo-types jiving to Girls Aloud, while being careful not to split their skinny jeans at the seam. Avoid the back room unless you like topless older men, but Thursday nights are the stuff of student legend.

Thu–Sun, 10pm-4am;

£7–£8

Angels Café Bar

127 Hurst Street

(0121) 622 4880

'Come on little devil/ Be my little angel', sang The Cult back in 1987. So hot that it's flaming (literally), Angels Café Bar is on fire with scenesters both young and old alike. Cool tunes and trendy climes make for a sweet yet spicy evening, and the sexy barmen definitely put a tick in our box (we wish). Smack in the middle of Brum's gay village, few bar crawls through this part of town are going to pass Angels by. Regular and generous drinks offers only serve to sweeten the deal, and ensure a swift descent into gloriously bad behaviour. This angelic haven will get your hell fires going.

Times vary

£5 after 11pm

Route 2

139–147 Hurst Street

(0121) 622 3366

Longstanding bar-cum-club that's busiest on Monday nights with their so-called 'pink pounder'. Unusually popular with lesbians and older guys, as well as fresher-faced, uni types. Except the local uni's LGBT who presumably thought another social at Nightingale would be pushing it. Expect plenty of Madonna, before the so-called r 'n' b 'hits' unfortunately take over. Good for cruising, but don't stare too long or someone may get jealous. Floors tend to be sticky, as do the men. All in all, good fun if you're drunk, ironically amusing when sober.

Mon & Thu-Sat, 7pm–2am;

Tue-Wed & Sun, 7pm–11pm

OTHER

Village Inn and Hotel

152 Hurst Street

(0121) 622 4742

One of the oldest venues on Hurst Street has had a makeover, and it's come out looking fresh as a daisy, unlike many of the regulars who were probably around when Quentin Crisp was in his prime. Four nights a week, the Inn's resident queen, Mrs Mills, presents karaoke, cabaret or bingo in her inimitable style with cash for the winners. Spend your prize on a discreet rendezvous at the hotel upstairs. Good for a swift one in the afternoon.

Mon-Wed, 12pm–11pm; Thu-Sat, 12pm–2am; Sun, 12pm–12.30am

Beds, £40

Shop

Shop

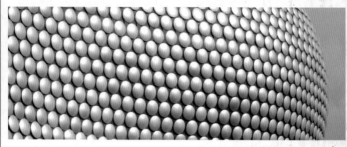

Welcome to Shop

You'll be pleased to hear that you can leave your orienteering skills at home if you plan to hit Brum's shops. Everywhere you need is within a credit card's swipe of New Street and the Bullring cunningly links it all up. For re-vamping your rekkid collection, **Swordfish Records (14 Temple Street, 0121 633 4859)** is one of the remaining independents and deserving of your money. If you like Elizabeth Duke jewellery off the back of a lorry, the **Bullring Indoor Market (Edgbaston Street)** should be on your route. **Selfridges (Bullring, 08708 377 377)** is king for a blow-out on payday and has tonnes of labels to browse longingly. Finally, the award for the most random shop goes to **The Moseley Emporium (116 Alcester Road 0121 449 3441)**. Most of the tat's been there long enough to go in and out of fashion several times over.

Top five bits of tourist tat to buy in Birmingham

Mini bronze bull – As a momento of having your picture taken next to it, on it, under it.

Imitation metal tool – Industry built this city but we doubt they used one of these in the process.

Blues/Villa footie shirt – Why not attract abuse everywhere you go.

Shakespeare hat, mug, pen, etc. He only lived down the road and we're gonna milk it.

Selfridge's giant smartie – Just pull one off the side, no one'll know.

Top five shops to bag a bargain in

Primark – Child labour? That fake leather jacket looks too damn good for us to care.

Vintage Warehouse – Secondhand tat with ominous stains removed.

The Works – A glorified jumble sale with cheap books, games and musical instruments galore.

Urban Outfitters – Wait for the sales then ravage those attractive young sales assistants .

Home Bargains – Ikea for chavs, but handy for everyone else.

DEPARTMENT STORES

Selfridges
Bullring
(0800) 123 400

Department store for those with new, old or daddy's money to play with. Whether it's lipstick, a kitchen appliance or a pair of socks, it'll have a designer label attached. Although strictly part of the Bullring, this is a world for another class of Brummies. The open-plan design is unmistakably Selfridges and they've even bred their own staff. Suspicious glances that say 'do you really think you belong here, mortal?' are just part of their art of intimidation. And the outside looks like it's covered in giant smarties.
🕑 *Mon–Fri, 10am–8pm; Sat, 9am–8pm; Sun, 10.30am–5pm*

The Mailbox
61–63 Wharfside Street
(0121) 632 1000

With an exclusive array of upmarket shops, restaurants, café-bars, hotels and 24hr parking, The Mailbox is the most prestigious location for shopping and lifestyle in Brum. Harvey Nicks, Emporio Armani and Hugo Boss are just a few of the heavyweight stylish stores you can expect to find here, as well as top spas and salons for some post-purchase pampering. And if you can't bear to remove your nose from the swish shop windows, you can always momentarily rest yourself and your wallet at the Ramada or the Malmaison.
🕑 *Mon–Wed, 10am–6pm; Thu–Sat, 10am–7pm; Sun, 11am–5pm; restaurants, Mon–Sun, 10am–late*

SHOPPING CENTRES

Birmingham Bullring
(0121) 632 1500

Crammed full of teenagers with screaming babies in triple pushchairs, and with its temperature eternally lurking round boiling point regardless of the season, the Bullring is still the pride and joy of Birmingham. Whatever retail indulgence it is that you've come for, you're liable to find it here, but the endless queues and rugby scrums at the bottom of the escalator will leave you bed-ridden for a week. Selfridges devotees have a separate entrance so as to avoid besmirching their designer vestments with the DNA of the masses.
🕑 *Mon–Fri, 9.30am–8pm; Sat, 9am–8pm; Sun, 11am–5pm*

Birmingham's most prestigious location
Exclusive shops
Restaurants
Café bars
Hotels
24 hour parking

Harvey Nichols • Emporio Armani • Hugo Boss • Fat Face • Toni & Gu

The Mailbox Wharfside Street Birmingham B1 1XL 0121 632 1000
www.mailboxlife.com

The Mailbox®
where else

Bar Room Bar • Gourmet Burger Kitchen • Nando's • Bar Estilo • Zizzi

Shop

MARKETS

Bullring Markets
Edgbaston Street
(0121) 464 8349

The only street in Birmingham containing everything your heart could ever desire, at cheaper-than-discount-chips prices. Get your fruit, veg, and ex-Army thermal underwear from the outdoor stalls. Move into the world-famous rag market for fancy dress, Action Men, and the carnivore heaven of the meat and fish stalls. Apart from saving your hard-earned cashish, the joke-cracking, Brummie stallholders beat spotty supermarket checkout boys any day.

Open market and rag market, Tue & Thu–Sat, 9am–5pm; Indoor market, Mon–Sat, 9am–5.30pm

Swordfish Records
14 Temple Street
(0121) 633 4859

One of the few remaining independent record shops in town. Anything too 'weird' for the high street chains is likely to be found somewhere in their indie, rock, metal or dance sections. The staff may not wear branded T-shirts and everything's a bit dusty but hey, that's cool man, you're indie now. The whole place is covered in posters for gigs near and far – near in this case being the Academy, whose gigs they sell tickets for. Get up-to-date on the latest nu-alt-electro-folk-metal sensation and do your bit for the indie kids of the future. Your carefully-spent pennies will help to save Swordfish from the corporate sharks.

Mon–Sat, 10am–6pm

MUSIC

Hard to Find Records
Vinyl House, 10 Upper Gough Street
(0121) 687 7777

You might have noticed that we like a good name here at Itchy, mostly because from time to time they provide us with some sort of cheap gag. But we can't really make anything of this one because the name really is just about the best way to describe the place. It really is hard to find proper old-fashioned records these days, and down here they've got all the rarities covered. Just to hammer the point home, they've also made their shop quite difficult to find, so have a peep at Multimap before you head out.

Mon–Sat, 10am–6pm

Temple Records
83 Bull Street
(0121) 236 9170

If you ignore the odd, over-emotional mid-teen emos hanging out by the door, pressing their pale little noses against the cold hard glass hoping that someone inside will take pity on their traumatic young lives and throw them a Panic! At The Disco CD, you'll soon realise that this record shop is a bit of a gem. For any true worshippers of rarities, limited editions or hard-to-finds that you're after, this is the altar to bow down before. They feature a huge collection of everything from alternative to hip hop, punk and dance, though anyone after The Fray is probably best off sticking to buying music in Tesco.

Mon–Sat, 9am–6pm

Zavvi
Union Gallery, Broadmead
(0117) 929 7798

We thought Zavvi was the cool Asian guy out of *Spooks*, but apparently it is what a music shop becomes after it loses its virginity. Sometime last year, all the Virgin Megastores in the world spontaneously turned green and became Zavvis, a transition all the more remarkable for the fact that almost no one noticed. In fairness that's probably because very little actually changed. They still do a nice range of discounts on popular albums, and Zavvi gets special brownie points for its listening points where you can scan in any CD and listen to excerpts.
☻ *Mon–Wed, 8.30am–6.30pm; Thu, 8.30am–7pm; Fri–Sat, 8.30am–6.30pm; Sun, 11am–5pm*

SHOES

Schuh
Level 1, Bullring
(0121) 643 9308

Aren't the people at Schuh clever by confusing us all? It's pronounced 'shoe', which, er, is exactly what they sell. The place is so packed with shoes you'll have to wedge yourself in with a horn. At every turn is yet another collection of the coolest footwear on the block, some so outrageous they'd make MC Hammer weep. Whether you're suited and booted or chaste and laced, you'll find something to fit. And if anyone tries to knock this shoe shrine, just tell them to schuh.
☻ *Mon–Fri, 9.30am–8pm; Sat, 9am–8pm; Sun, 11am–5pm*

BOOKS

WH Smith
East Mews, City Centre
0121 643 0052

The WH stands for, 'We Have (everything)'. Okay, so we didn't think that one through.
☻ *Mon–Fri, 9am–5.30pm; Sat, 9am–6pm; Sun, 11am–5pm*

Waterstone's
128 New Street
(0121) 631 4333

What a relaxing name for a bookshop. Sounds like it should be featured in *Around The World in 80 Gardens*, but with books. And cards.
☻ *Mon–Tue & Thu–Fri, 9am–6.30pm; Wed, 9.30am–6.30pm; Sat, 9am–6pm; Sun, 11am–5pm*

UNISEX CLOTHING

A2
9 Ethel Street
(0121) 643 3989

In the current climate of a new Primark causing mile long queues and heavyweight catfights, and own-brand supermarket clothes shopping becoming a certified addiction (apparently), Itchy finds A2 something of a relief. Call us snobs, but it's reassuring now and then to know that foolish sorts can still spend £60 on a T-shirt or £100 on a hoodie with 'your mum's a twat' emblazoned across the front. A2 is perfect if you're feeling flush and don't fancy battling the hordes slugging it out for the last sweatshop-stitched size 12.
☻ *Mon–Fri, 10am–6pm; Sun, 12pm–4.30pm*

Shop

Primark

18 New Street
(0121) 643 5978

A jam-packed death trap, Primark is more like a full body workout than a shopping experience. Three floors of home goodies and ethically dubious, dirt cheap clothes that melt in the washing machine play host to daily rugby scrums. Pram-wielding parents are at the top of the Primark food chain, so borrow a baby if possible. Otherwise, go early or suffer the direst of consequences. However, since thousands of Brummies pour in day in, day out, Primark are definitely doing something right. Selling sexy leather jackets for less than a tenner, for instance.

🕑 *Mon–Wed, 9am–7pm; Thu, 9am–8pm; Fri–Sat, 9am–7pm; Sun, 11am–5pm*

Urban Outfitters

5–7 Corporation Street
(0121) 633 2920

If you refer to yourself as a 'fashionista' or talk about 'last season' in a non-weather context, Urban Outfitters could be right up your fashionable street. Since it crossed the pond from America, they've got British talent running the show. Alongside their own collection, there are designer and vintage ranges, very swish but predictably overpriced. The perfect example of their pleasing take on fashion is their 'I'm not a Smug Twat' bag, in response to the not-so-eco, eco-friendly bag by designer Anya Hindmarch. If you know who she is, get your Vogue-reading arse down here.

🕑 *Mon–Wed & Fri–Sat, 10am–7pm; Thu, 11am–8pm; Sun, 11am–5pm*

TK Maxx

Ground Floor, Bullring
(0121) 643 7302

Ever wonder how your peers can afford to wear designer threads while you're still searching the high street for knock-offs? Pay TK Maxx just one swift visit and all will be explained. Actually, it won't be that swift, since it takes some serious trawling through the racks to find something that's your size, your style and doesn't have brand names splattered all over it like emulsion on a decorator's overalls. It's stacked with big-name brands at half their normal price, plus this one's a superstore, so there's more designer goodness than the Beckhams' walk-in wardrobe.

🕑 *Mon–Fri, 9am–8pm; Sat, 9am–5pm; Sun, 11am–5pm*

SECONDHAND

Vintage Warehouse

82–85 Digbeth High Street

(0121) 643 8989

Vintage is the new way of saying 'old and crap'. If you like 'old and crap' clothes you may want to visit the 'Old and Crap Warehouse' in Digbeth. If you've got a few days to spare it can be worth rooting through the stupidly crammed rails, but expect hundreds of pasty-skinned 'alternative types' buying skinny ties to wear to the discotheque that night. You'll also find 'emo' haircuts by the dozen, weird assistants and you'll get charged double what you would in your local Oxfam, without a penny going to charity.

Mon–Fri, 9am–6pm; Sat, 11am–5pm

OTHER

Blue Banana

The Pallasades, New Street

(0121) 665 6289

Once upon a time, someone probably had a vibrant and exciting vision for the Pallasades, but the Blue Banana sign is about as bright as this shopping centre gets nowadays. A refreshing break from the pound shops, Blue Banana sits on the more alternative side of the scales. Stars, studs, skinny jeans and skulls galore. Plus T-shirts bearing the name of every guitar-playing or eyeliner-wearing band in existence. With its own in-house piercing studio, (and a special £5 on weekdays offer to boot), self-induced holes are another speciality.

Mon–Sat, 9.30am–6pm; Sun, 11am–5pm

Yo Yo

7 Ethel Street

(0121) 633 3073

'Why don't we try flogging on some ropey clobber at hefty prices?' said Mrs Yoyo, voicing another of her crazy ideas. 'I've got a load of nasty polyester stuff from the 70s that I never wear'. 'That's ridiculous' said Mr Yoyo, 'no one would pay such prices for old shit', but just how wrong could he be? Well to be honest, no one knows, as Mr and Mrs Yoyo don't actually exist. But considering the number of yeppies in here looking for an 'original piece', we guess he'd be even wronger than granny porn. Okay, it's overpriced tat, but it's the place to be seen, and the assistants are always happy to 'help'.

Mon–Fri, 10am–6pm; Sun, 12pm–4pm

Oasis Market

112–114 Corporation Street

(0121) 710 5439

A four-storey labyrinth of alternative clothes stalls, piercing/tattoo studios and a hair salon. The perfect place to pick up that rubber nurse's uniform or 10-inch heeled goth boots you've been after. Or just have a wander through the maze of stairs and corridors amidst wispy hippy skirts and baggy trousers, chequered tops and leopard print drainpipe jeans. If plain Converse are too last year for you, be the coolest kid on the block with polka dot, pinstripe or floral numbers, not forgetting neon laces for that extra heartbroken emo touch. Angst-ridden teenagers, we know the world hates you, but welcome home.

Mon–Fri, 10am–5.30pm; Sat, 10am–6pm

Shop

The Art Lounge

The Mailbox, 28–30 Wharfside Street

(0121) 685 2555

If your living room walls are about as interesting as a padded cell, The Art Lounge can save you from the asylum with a painting, photograph or even sculpture to brighten up your den. They have something from every period of art you never understood at school, plus pieces far too risqué for innocent young minds to handle. Those who never even progressed from crayon to chalk will appreciate the advice of staff at the gallery, without even a whisper of 'uncultured oaf'. Waste some time at work before you go and browse the collections on the website, after reading their very handy buying guide.

 Mon-Sat, 10am–6pm; Sun, 11am–5pm

The Moseley Emporium

116 Alcester Road, Moseley

(0121) 449 3441

This rickety, tumbledown shop takes Moseley's bohemian reputation into the realms of very weird. On the top floor, a six-foot statue of a naked woman sits next to a reprint of the 'Creation' from the Sistine chapel, and the staircase is lined with skulls (which given the skeletal state of the staff can't help but make you wonder how strict they are about tardiness of a morning). The three floors' worth of goods doesn't necessarily justify the 'emporium' tag, however, with the strange, strange artefacts on sale making you feel like you're shopping in a haunted house, it's still well worth a visit.

 Mon-Sat, 10am–5.30pm

Home Bargains

84–88 High Street, Harborne

(0121) 426 6247

The name of this penny-saving mecca is but a clue to the wonders that lurk behind its sliding doors. Brand name products to clean everything in your life including you, as well as your house, toilet and probably pet snake. You'll find everything here that you would in a big supermarket, but the bargain bit's the key. It'll probably be about half the price that you'd normally pay. For non-cleaning fans, there's toys, furniture and food galore. Orange squash for 17p, containing 2% real fruit. OK, so maybe you can pass up juice that tastes like dishwater, but at least you can get enough washing-up liquid for 30p to run a new sink full.

 Mon-Sat, 9am–6pm; Sun, 10am–4pm

Three White Walls Gallery

Level 3, The Mailbox, Wharfside Street

(0121) 632 1282

Three White Walls offers an absorptive forum in which the divide between life and art is blurred. The minimalistic and simple presentation of the regular solo-installations, attracting the best new talents in paint, glass and sculpture, at once isolates and defines the quality of the works displayed in the most lucid manner. We have no idea what we have just said, but it sounded great, didn't it? Moving on, you'd think at £1,500 a pop for the exhibits they could afford to brighten the place up a bit. All it wants is a dado rail, some net curtains and maybe a Toby jug or two.

 Mon-Wed, 10am–6pm; Thu-Sat, 10am–7pm; Sun, 11am–5pm

Nice Things

545 Bristol Road, Selly Oak

(0121) 472 6086

Naming your shop after two of the most bland, non-descript words in the English language doesn't strike us as the best marketing ploy. But then they are marketing to the 'what-evaaa' generation. It's what's on the inside that counts and they've got that right. Perfect for last-minute presents and fancy dress gear that you'll only wear once anyway. Nice Things is the type of place you enter for one thing and leave with bags of other stuff you don't need. Students get a 5% discount, barely worth it to working folk but worth at least another 'comedy' mug to those on the last legs of their loan.

🕒 *Mon–Fri, 9am–6pm; Sat, 9am–5.30pm*

Shared Earth

87 New Street

(0121) 633 0151

The Birmingham branch of this fair trade company is full of hand-carved ethnic-y goods that you can easily pass off as presents for your more environmentally-friendly mates. Goes without saying of course that you could buy most of it for half the price somewhere else, but knowing your new wall hanging was woven by a fairly-paid African child is bound to make it much nicer to look at, as well as being easy on the conscience. With lots of products made from recycled goods, you would be factually correct in saying Shared Earth is full of rubbish. But that wouldn't be very ethical now, would it?

🕒 *Mon–Sat, 10am–6pm; Sun, 11am–4pm*

Nostalgia & Comics

14–16 Smallbrook Queensway

(0121) 643 0143

With its phasers set to maximum and more photon torpedoes on board than you can shake a Klingon battle-mace at, Nostalgia and Comics offers the best Earth has to offer in sci-fi and anime at low low Martian prices. So if you could translate this into Klingon, have visited that site where it lists the religious affiliations of all Marvel superheroes (which, we've, ahem, heard about from our geeky mates) and know how many moons the Ice Planet Hoff has (or if the patronising tone of this review has you reaching for your lightsabers), then beam on down there, Scotty.

🕒 *Mon–Wed, 9.30am–5.30pm; Thu–Sat, 9.30am–6pm; Sun, 11am–4pm*

Shop

Zen

4 The Waters Edge, Brindleyplace

(0121) 643 3933

If in this, or in any other plane of existence, you have or have had a penchant for the magical and the arcane, then you and your aura should find peace in this here realm. With an enchanting range of herbal remedies, healing crystals, and a resident medium hidden behind a veil of smoke, Zen promises a fix for all of your karmic maladies and other spiritual/energy flow crises. Herbal remedies that perhaps do a little more than just remedy can also be picked up. An otherworldly staff of Wiccans and Pagans completes this lovely new age patchwork.

☾ *Mon–Thu & Sun, 10am–10.30pm; Fri, 10am–11pm; Sat, 9.30am–11.30pm*

The Works

137 New Street

(0121) 643 3092

Seriously discounted books jostle for space with art materials, greeting cards and old biddies looking for books about knitting. They do a nice line in toys for the grandkids too, plus cheap, plastic musical instruments (which will, we imagine, be of far more interest to the Itchy reader). It seems some shoppers are a little over-enthusiastic – when we went there was a guitar with its neck snapped off discarded on the floor. If you're looking to learn a new craft or pick up a cheap book for a long train journey, The Works is your best bet. Alternatively, entertain fellow passengers and learn the new craft while on the train.

☾ *Mon–Sat, 8am–7pm; Sun, 10am–5pm*

Out & About

Out & About

Welcome to Out & About

If you're not a museum type, never fear, there's plenty more here. Good ol' Alton Towers is the nearest theme park but for an adrenaline rush in the city head for the **IMAX cinema at Millennium Point (Curzon Street, 0121 202 2222)**. Probably not the best date though, those 3D glasses don't have quite the same effect as beer goggles. If it's a rainy day, **Cadbury World (Lindon Road, 0121 451 4159)** is a safe option. Unless, that is, you're already morbidly obese, in which case it could be the nail in the very wide coffin. If laughter is your favourite medicine the **Glee Club (Arcadian, Hurst Street, 0870 241 5093)** will leave you smacked up for days. If you're looking for a shot of culture, the charming **Midland Arts Centre in Cannon Hill Park (Russell Road, Moseley, 0121 440 6122)** has theatre, art, films and really good hot chocolate for the interval.

Top five summer activities

West Midland Safari Park – Excellent alternative to that Kenyan extravaganza you had planned.

Cannon Hill Park – Get an ice cream, feed the ducks, ignore the perves hiding in the trees.

Lickey Hills Country Park – The hills are alive with the sound of yam yams.

Sutton Park – Come and see how far you can throw a Frisbee.

The Electric – The weather might let you down but a good indie film never will.

Top five winter activities

German Christmas market – Glühwein and a merry-go-round, what a combo.

Winterbourne Botanic Garden – The clue's in the name.

The Rep – Go for the Christmas panto and heckle the Z-list celebrity in the 'starring' role.

Cadbury World – Cold weather is the perfect excuse to binge on chocolate – you need the extra insulation.

Star City – Take the kids on a rainy day, you can lose them for hours.

Itchy's Dictionary of *Dahling!*

EVER FELT THAT THE CULTURE-SAVVY SEEM TO DWELL ON A HIGHER INTELLECTUAL PLANE THAN THE REST OF US? WELL NEVER FEAR – BEHIND THEIR LUVVIE LINGO, REFINED-SOUNDING FOLK HAVE THE SAME THOUGHTS, HOPES AND FEARS AS US CRUDE PROLETARIANS. HAVE A PEEP AT ITCHY'S THESP THESAURUS TO FIND OUT WHAT THEY'RE REALLY ON ABOUT.

ON THEATRE

'I found the final act deeply moving.' – *The end was just like Last of the Mohicans.*

'His sense of comic timing left something to be desired.' – *I've had funnier episodes of food poisoning.*

'I felt the costumes were rather avant-garde.' – *I could almost see Juliet's nipples in that corset.*

ON MUSIC

'I don't much care for their notion of ensemble.' – *I'm going to piss in a bottle and throw it at the drummer.*

'I've always had a sense of vocation about the arts.' – *Why don't we start a band? I've got an old cowbell I stole from school and you could play the harmonica.*

ON DANCING

'Oh my, I'm all left feet this evening!' – *We both know that I was dry-humping your leg just then, but let's never speak of it again, eh?*

'Nothing like a foxtrot to aid one's constitution.' – *I'm shagged. Where's the bar?*

ON WINE

'This wine's really got legs.' – *And I won't when I've had enough of it.*

'A young and bold number, with zesty notes of rosemary and field mushroom.' – *This one was the second cheapest on the menu.*

ON ART GALLERIES

'I find the figurative liberties of proto-classical sculpture highly diverting.' – *Hee hee, look at the massive wanger on that statue. I wonder if they sell replicas in the shop.*

Illustration by Si Clarke

Out & About

CINEMAS

AMC Cinemas
Broadway Plaza, 220 Ladywood Middleway, Five Ways
(0870) 755 5657

Generally, there's not much to distinguish one cinema from the next; they're soulless look-alikes with overpriced popcorn and ASBO teens too young to go anywhere else. The AMC, however, is a small cut above the rest. It's fairly clean and cheap, plus there's the chance to show off just what a sad film geek you are by identifying all the quotes in the entrance. As an added bonus, the oversized sofa seats are perfect for the boring bits in *Titanic*-length features.

🕐 *Mon–Thu, 11.30am–11pm; Fri–Sat, 11.30am–12am; Sun, 11.30am–10pm*
🎟 *£3.50; £5 after 6pm*

Birmingham Hippodrome Theatre
Hurst Street
(0870) 730 1234

One of the city's oldest theatres has stayed drastic, modern thanks to a *Changing Rooms*-style makeover. As far as we can tell, new shows seem to launch just about every night, with musicals, stand-up, dance and new productions of classic plays on rotation. If you want to see a big West End production outside of the capital, the Hippodrome's a safe bet. Aside from the main theatre, the smaller Patrick Centre showcases dance and performing arts productions. Fans of warbling and wailing from the West might like to know that the Welsh National Opera visit here regularly.

🕐 *Box office, Mon–Sat, 9.30am–8pm*

The Electric Cinema
47–49 Station Street
(0121) 643 7279

Back when it was still called 'the pictures' the UK's oldest working cinema opened, and it's still the best in the city. Showing a wider choice of flicks than your average 12-screener, this film experience has a class that you don't find all so often these days. Tickets start at four quid, or you could go the whole hog and get the 'Text A Waiter' service. Your order is delivered right to your sofa, with absinthe from a fountain top of the menu. Every settee in the place is named after a star of the silver screen, which means that Laurel and Hardy are available to hire should you need a date for the night.

🕐 *Opens 30 minutes before first film*

Odeon
139 New Street
(0871) 224 4007

With a measly eight screens, this Odeon doesn't compare to the mother ships docked at the top of Broad Street. But, just opposite the train station, it's way more convenient, and last time we checked you could only watch one film at a time anyway. As you might expect, big name blockbusters tend to dominate, but pleasingly there are also some late screenings of the classics. Flash your student card for a discount or, if yours expired in 1982, family tickets can save you a bob or two. Smuggle in your own snacks and buy a meal for two later with what you saved on popcorn.

🕐 *Check website for film times*

COMEDY

Jongleurs Comedy Club

Quayside Tower, Broad Street

(0870) 787 0707

Jongleurs are responsible for bringing Harry Enfield and Lee Evans to your screens and they're still managing to bring us the finest of rib-ticklers. To top up your comedy appetites, they'll bring food and buckets of alcohol straight to your table. If the warm-up acts leave you with the chills, you can throw some hilarious shapes in Bar Risa after the show.

☺ Thu–Sat, show starts 8.30pm (last entry 8pm); bar closes, 3am

🍴 Fish & chips, £5.95

🎫 £7.95

🎟 £9/£13/£16

The Carling Academy Birmingham

52–54 Dale End

(0121) 262 3000

Beer company sponsorship means the Academy attracts bands of international fame as well as up-and-coming hot stuff. Flip side of the coin, only said beer is on tap, to the tune of extortion, and the ropey teenage club nights amuse Itchy no end. We once wandered past the Saturday night fallout and were asked if we were emo. Was this a reference to our emotional state or music taste? We didn't stop long enough to decide. Aside from a couple of awkward moments with boys wearing eyeliner, the quality of the acts means the Academy can be a place of happy memories.

☺ Times vary

LIVE MUSIC

Barfly

78 Digbeth High Street (behind The Sanctuary)

(0121) 633 8311

The Barfly is in Digbeth. Digbeth is the 'hip little quarter' just off the town centre, the Camden of the Midlands if you like. The Barfly is a hip little venue for hip little gigs by hip little bands. However, whilst the bands are usually little, unfortunately the 'hip' bit is occasionally more like 'my hip is so loose, it may need replacing'. Oh, it also smells and the floor glistens with a concoction of snakebite, sick and saliva.

☺ Sun–Thu, 7.30pm–11.30pm; Fri, 7.30pm–2am; Sat, 7.30pm–3am; Sun, 7.30pm–11.30pm

🎟 Club nights, £3–£7

The Glee Club

The Arcadian Centre, Hurst Street

(0870) 241 5093

Gig venue by week, comedy club by weekend. Take some Itchy advice and book online, 'cos you'll need your pennies for the bar. The Glee is a bit of a double-edged sword. It hosts some brilliant entertainment but doors close half an hour before anyone takes to the stage. So you're forced to pay their drinks prices all night. That's once you've elbowed everyone in your row in the face and knocked over the drink that just cost them a week's wages. Still, brave the social discomfort and slightly oldie crowd and you're in for a very funny night, whatever the bill.

☺ Tue–Sun, 7.30pm–12am; food, Tue–Sun from 7.30pm

Out & About

The Roadhouse

Wharfside Leisure Complex, Lifford Lane, Stirchley

(0121) 624 2920

Any music venue worth its salt has a grimy history of struggle and strife, all in the name of the blues. A crowd of Stirchleyans got the blues when their local closed down, and they found that park benches just didn't have the same allure. So, like all good crusaders, they took charge and turned a leisure centre's bar into The Roadhouse. These days they put on live music every night of the week and only charge on three of them. Local favourites get a regular slot and you never know what you might be subjected to on open mic nights.

- Mon–Sat, 7pm–11pm;
Sun, 12pm–10.30pm
- Prices vary

Symphony Hall

ICC, Broad Street

(0121) 780 3333

If you're a student, chances are the only time you'll visit the Symphony Hall will be to pick up your degree. Unless you're a fan of 10cc, UB40 or Dr Hook that is. Yes, it's often where dad rockers play at huge expense when they've got a tax bill to pay. Perhaps we're doing you and the hall an injustice. 10cc are pretty good after all. If strings are more your thing, book an evening in with the Symphony Orchestra. You can always leave at half time. Or failing that, you can get steaming during the interval in a bid to make the second half go by a bit quicker.

- Box Office, Mon–Fri, 10am–6pm
(concert nights, 8pm); Sat, 10am–8pm;
Sun, 2pm–8pm

MUSEUMS

Think Tank Science Museum

Curzon Street

(0121) 202 2222

Buildings built to commemorate the turn of the century seem doomed to failure, making Brummies all the more smug that Millennium Point actually receives some visitors. The museum is made up of nine zones with more exhibits, videos and experiments than even the most hyperactive child could get their hands on. The IMAX cinema is just as fun, but expect to leave a little dizzy. The third attraction is the huge planetarium with plenty of space-related delights, but remember to book well in advance.

- Mon–Sun, 10am–5pm (last admission 4pm)
- Think Tank and IMAX, £15; concs, £11

THEATRE

The Birmingham Repertory Theatre

Centenary Square, Broad Street

(0121) 236 4455

Don't let the name put you off – old men in tights reciting Shakespeare are a rarity here. Joe Bloggs who thinks the theatre is for 'posh types' is their target. Fairy tale fantasy or gritty realism, you can bet your interval ice-cream that it will be superb. As they are also a working theatre company it's a one stop shop from rehearsal to the big night. They've also got The Door, a studio theatre showing work by new writers.

- Box office opening times, performance days, 10am–8pm; non-performance days, 10am–6pm

Glamourous

Albany House, 27–35 Hurst Street

(0121) 622 4770

So you're done up likc it's opening night at *The Rocky Horror Picture Show*. Eyeliner? Check. Hairspray-styled beehive wig? Check. Electric blue sling-backs? Got 'em. You have the look, baby, but where to go? Head to Glamourous to join in the fun and frolics with the most fabulous camp cabaret and best live entertainment this side of *An Evening with Kylie* on the television (that's the living side, daahling). Yes, don't stay at home with a remote and a bag of Walkers (even the posh kind), when every night of the week at Glamourous is overflowing with gloriously camp mayhem.

🕙 *Mon–Thu, 6pm–4am; Fri–Sun, 4pm–4am*

🎫 *Free entry*

Birminghams no1 GAY cabaret bar

featuring the best drag & cabaret acts from around the UK

Albany House, Hurst Street, Birmingham. B5

www.glamourous-showbar.com

Out & About

GALLERIES

Barber Institute of Fine Arts
University of Birmingham Edgbaston
(0121) 414 7333

Despite sitting on the edge of the city's biggest University campus, most students are too busy binge drinking, dodging lectures, swapping STDs and moaning about top-up fees to visit what is one of Britain's best small art galleries. Which is a shame, because featuring works from Rembrandt, Turner, Degas, Monet, van Gogh and Rodin, and Pre-Raphaelite art, it's well worth a look. Note to women and cross-dressing men: don't wear heels. Your footsteps will echo around the whole building.
Mon–Sat, 10am–5pm; Sun, 12pm–5pm

BMAG
Chamberlain Square
(0121) 303 2834

Boasting the world's largest collection of Pre-Raphaelite paintings, amongst other things, the BMAG is a sanctum for those who like pictures and that. Offering a refreshing and cultured interlude from a day shoplifting at the Bullring, the Gallery's exquisite Edwardian tea rooms will have culture vultures holding their little fingers up in delight as you sup on delicate pastries and dainties. With a programme of fun events for kids, the Museum caters for all and won't be snubbed by younger (or older) visitors who just want to see swords, skeletons and dino bones.
Mon–Thu, 10am–5pm; Fri, 10.30am–5pm; Sat, 10am–5pm; Sun 12.30pm–5pm

Ikon Gallery
Brindley Place
(0121) 248 0708

If you feel like doing something really radical then pop on down to the Ikon Gallery where you can rest assured you won't feel at all welcome. Not only will the building remind you of the pain of school trips, but the staff are intimidating and the place quite frankly has a funny smell to it. But, if we gloss over these few modest downsides, the Ikon Gallery is still one of Birmingham's proudest assets drawing an impressive register of international contemporary artists displaying some of their most provocative work. Last time we went there were some rotting apples. As we said... it's radical.
Tue–Sun, 11am–6pm

The Halcyon Gallery
International Convention Centre, Broad Street
(0121) 248 8484

Situated in the Symphony Hall and featuring a wide range of reproduction and original artworks, the Halcyon Gallery is a veritable El Dorado for those who have more culture than a pot of Yakult and more lolly than a mint choc chip Feast. Artistry of this exalted quality doesn't come cheap, however, with individual pieces costing well into the hundreds and upwards. However, they can't sting you for looking, can they? Come on down, dust off your monocle and velvet jacket, and have a gander. If you like the look of something and you're feeling a bit flush you could always take out another mortgage.
Mon–Sat, 10am–6pm; Sun, 11am–5pm

SPORT

Bowlplex

Broadway Plaza, Five Ways
(0121) 410 5888

Always much more fun if you get those buffers put along the edges of the lanes. When you're done hurling balls down the alleys, you can move on to the pool tables or dance zone. And before you ask, it's called a 'zone' because of the blinding strobe lighting and the fat DJ on the decks. Oh and don't forget the big screen sports action that you'll regularly find here. If you want to watch the footy, we reckon you should stay at home. If you've not got round to setting up your bowling zone yet, then this place'll do.

🕒 *Mon–Sun, 10am–late*

EVENTS AND FESTIVALS

Fierce Festival

(0121) 244 8084

This month-long arts festival is an assault on the senses aimed at anyone who's not afraid of the unusual. The 2007 festival included a kids' orchestra playing instruments made out of vegetables, a transvestite giving haircuts at a local salon and a mass arm-wrestling competition. In Fierce's eyes, they're all art forms. Theatre makes up a good chunk of the programme, and whatever the event, they guarantee you'll leave with a smile on your face. Whether it's a smile of amusement or one of slight bewilderment is a different matter though. Still, can't ask for more than that.

🕒 *Annually, May–June; various venues*

German Christmas Market

Victoria Square

If you can't make it to the continent to buy tacky German souvenirs and eat marzipan 'til you're sick, here's an acceptable alternative. Stalls selling Christmas decorations, jewellery and assorted pointless ornaments fill the square, with a mini outdoor pub being a highlight. If it gets to December and you've yet to find that perfect gift for Auntie Noreen, a stall here has the answer. A toy reindeer singing 'We Wish you a Merry Christmas' is sure to go down a treat. Singletons beware: loved up couples toasting their blissful happiness are everywhere so take a sympathetic mate and OD on glühwein.

🕒 *15th November–23rd December, 10am–9pm*
🎟 *Free*

Laters

You Snooze, You Lose

MISSING OUT ON LATE-NIGHT FUN BECAUSE YOUR GROOVY TRAIN IS STUCK IN LAZY TOWN? WANNA BE A MEMBER OF THE WIDE AWAKE CLUB, BUT YOUR DOZY HEAD FEELS HEAVIER THAN MALLETT'S MALLET? YOU NEED ITCHY'S MINI A-TO-ZED OF WAYS TO STAY AWAKE FOR DAYS…

If you don't want to set foot in the Land of Nod for a whole 24 hours, preparation must begin at breakfast time. If, like us, you like to kick your day off with a Weetabix or two, you'll know that dried-up cereal is one of the stickiest, most viciously viscous substances known to man. Smear a little porridge onto your eyelids and press them up towards your brows. Next, hold your head over the toaster to accelerate the drying process. Result: your peepers will be glued open permanently, or until it rains.

Worrying is a great way to stave off the sandman. Want to stay wired throughout a week-long holiday or festival? Go for an STD test just before things kick off. It'll be an agonising seven days before your results come through, during which time you won't sleep a wink.

Threadworms are known to be more active at night. Pick up your own wriggly-ass infestation by babysitting for your neighbourhood's grubbiest kids, then enjoy hours of sleeplessness courtesy of an intensely itchy bum. It's guaranteed you'll still be up at the – ahem – 'crack' of dawn.

Or, watch that kinky home video you discovered in your ma and pa's camcorder collection. Better than any horror film for making sure you'll never sleep again.

Illustration by Si Clarke

LATE-NIGHT SHOPPING

For late-night shopping in Brummingham it's all about those soulless shrines of consumerism: shopping centres. When you're curing the winter blues with some therapy of the retail kind you'll be bloody glad of that blast of hot air. **The Bullring (20 High Street, 0121 632 1500)** is the obvious starting point. Anyone near the railway station is gently pushed in the right direction via the escalators leading out of the station. It's open 'til 8pm from Monday to Saturday, and with 140 stores under one huge glass roof you'd be lucky to cover a floor. For the best out-of-town shopping head for the city. **Star City (32 Watson Road, 0121 328 9880)** is known for its 30-screen cinema but the shopping ain't half bad either. Doors are open 'til midnight seven days a week.

LATE-NIGHT DRINKING

With the 24-hour drinking laws, you'd think that drinking after hours would be easy. Well it is. Most of the bars around Hurst Street stay open 'til every dark corner has been used and abused. **Glamourous Show Bar (27–35 Hurst Street, 0121 622 4770)** is one of our faves, with regular cabaret shows and shocking stand-up. If that isn't your scene then the charming **Tap and Spile (10–15 Gas Street, 0121 632 5062)**

is open 'til the so-late-it's-early hour of 4am every day. This is the only place we've found where you can knock back a pint of real ale at three in the morning.

FAGS AT 4AM

If shisha's just not damaging enough for you, begin the late-night fag hunt. Two supermarkets in town stay open 'til the wee hours. The windows of **Costcutter (2–5 Suffolk Street Queensway)** by the New Street roundabout are plastered in neon signs advertising 'We Sell Alcohol Late' so the drinking can continue. There's also a **Select & Save (78 Hill Street, 0121 633 0268)** behind New Street Station. If you're a student heading home to Selly Oak, **Tesco Express (479 Bristol Road, 0845 677 9608)** can feed more than just your petrol habit.

POST CLUB ACTION

For a post-club wind-down we find a shisha pipe is just the ticket. Shame the government disagreed and caused most of them to close following the smoking ban. But **Ali Babas (628–630 Bristol Road, 0121 472 1144)** in Selly Oak refused to be beaten and just moved the whole operation outside. You can still have coffee and soft drinks inside but move to the heated garden out the back for the good stuff.

FOOD NOW!

When you've got the late night munchies and fancy chewing on something other than your own face, the city centre's got it sorted. If you've been out in Digbeth, **Salt'n'Pepper (88–89 Digbeth High Street, 0121 643 5086)** does more than just seasoning. They do the usual greasy delights, which should go a long way to preventing a hangover the next day. For post-gig refuelling, **Ocean Fish Bar (59 Dale End)** is a hop, skip and a trip from the Academy. Expect long queues of sweaty teenagers, but you know it'll be worth it when you've got those steaming chips in your clammy hands. **Mr Egg (22 Hurst Street, 0121 622 4344)** is an institution with clubbers. Resident in the gay quarter for longer than the saggiest trannies, Mr Egg's got it all, including an all-day-and-all-night breakfast.

OTHER LATE-NIGHT INDULGENCES

For late-night entertainment of an energetic kind, there's no two ways about it, there's Five Ways. **Bowlplex (Broadway Plaza, 0121 410 5880)** is open 'til late throughout the week with a disco and bar to bowl you over. The casino in the same complex and the nearby **Grosvenor (263 Broad Street, 0121 631 2414)** encourage frivolous betting throughout the night, rarely closing before 6am. If it's a late night film you're after, head to the **Odeon (139 New Street, 0871 224 4007)**.

Sleep

Sleep

SWANKY

City Inn

1 Brunswick Square, Brindleyplace

(0121) 643 1003

In that *Friends* episode, 'The One Where They Go To Birmingham', they stay here. 24-hour room service – they'll be there for you.

Rooms, from £150

Radisson SAS

12 Holloway Circus, Queensway

(0121) 654 6000

Should you be able to afford the torpedoing your credit card will take to stay at the Radisson, you'll have very little trouble finding the place. The outside is covered in glass so it's one giant, 39-storey mirror.

Rooms, from £135

Malmaison

The Mailbox, 1 Wharfside Street

(0121) 246 5000

If GCSE French serves us right, 'mal' means bad. So, despite being one of the top hotels in Brum, this is the Bad House. This conjures up all sort of images, none of them being an award-winning hotel.

Rooms, from £150 per night

Ramada

The Mailbox

(0121) 643 9344

Amazing; a hotel that fits into a post box. They manage to fit all kinds of other stuff in there too. Your hotel's on the 7th floor, and everything else you need's a lift ride away. Ramada-lama-ding-dong.

Rooms, from £60

Britannia Hotel

New Street

(0121) 631 3331

If you want to be first in line for Primark's new collection then sleeping here is going to be your only option. Up at 6am and roll out of the doors with your credit cards at the ready...

Rooms, from £79

Copthorne Hotel

Paradise Circus

(0121) 200 2727

'Centrally located' usually means Britain's busiest road runs through the lobby. Not here. It's close to everywhere but not right on top of anywhere. Oh and some bloke off *Ready Steady Cook* designed the restaurant menu.

Rooms, from £55

MID-RANGE

Jury's Inn

Broad Street

(0121) 606 9000

Did they call their hotel an inn to give it that rustic and homely feel, like it might be run by a lady called Sandra?

🛏 *Rooms, from £59*

Paragon Hotel

145 Alcester Street

(0121) 627 0627

Recent refurbishments mean the inside almost matches its grand, Grade II listed exterior. It's not in the city centre but only a stone's throw from Digbeth's clubs and pubs. Book on the net for good discounts.

🛏 *Rooms, from £45*

CHEAP

Birmingham Backpackers

58 Coventry Street, Digbeth

(0121) 440 2183

Your backpack's loaded and you're ready to go. Bahamas? Nah. Bolivia? Too far. Brazil? Too hot. Birmingham? Perfect.

🛏 *Beds, from £16; breakfast included*

Etap

1 Great Colmore Street

(0121) 622 7575

Only 10 minutes from New Street but right by a main road, so try and walk it and it'd probably be the last 10 minutes of your life. But even with the £4 taxi ride this is still one of the cheapest options in the city.

🛏 *Rooms, from £35*

Norfolk Hotel

267 Hagley Road

(0121) 454 8071

Naming your hotel after a place 160 miles from Birmingham city centre seems a bit silly. But we'll try not to hold that against this 3* haunt, full of businessmen and other fellas enjoying an evening away from home.

🛏 *Rooms, from £55; breakfast included*

Travel Lodge

230 Broad Street

(0121) 644 5266

Easy to stumble back to in the early hours as it's smack bang in the middle of the busiest clubbing street in Birmingham. A good night's sleep probably isn't as easy as the clubbers on the street below.

🛏 *Rooms, from £61*

Comfort Inn

Station Street

(0121) 643 1134

Practise the long jump off your train and you'll land at the Comfort Inn's door. Boasting 3 stars and 'interior corridors' as hotel services, you get the not-so-comforting picture.

🛏 *Rooms, from £49*

Lyby Guest House

14–16 Barnsley Road, Edgbaston

(0121) 429 4487

It's all in the name. Nowhere as cheap does 'lie by' the city. After enjoying a hearty breakfast, jump in a cab and you'll be central and ready to hit the shops, bars and restaurants in ten minutes.

🛏 *Rooms, from £15, breakfast included*

Itchy

We need hawk-eyed photographers to contribute their sparkling talents to the Itchy city guides and websites.

We want dynamic pictures of bars, pubs, clubs and restaurants in your city, as well as photos to represent the comedy, art, music, theatre, cinema and sport scenes.

If you're interested in getting involved, please send examples of your photography to: editor@itchymedia.co.uk, clearly stating which city you can work in. All work will be fully credited.

Calling all aspiring photographers

Useful info

Useful info

HAIR AND BEAUTY

Saks Hair and Beauty

Great Western Arcade

(0121) 233 9993

Should your locks need help, here they are.

☺ *Mon–Tue, 9am–6pm; Wed–Thu, 9am–8pm; Fri–Sat, 9am–6pm*

☻ *From £7*

Supercuts

80 New Street

(0121) 633 4541

The fast-food chain of hairdressers, you can walk in off the street and you know it'll be cheap. What you'll feel like when you gaze into the mirror the next morning is another story.

☺ *Mon–Sat, 9am–6pm; Sun, 11am–5pm*

The Spa at Birmingham College of Food, Tourism and Creative Studies

84 Newhall Street

(0121) 604 1020

Under full supervision, college students can treat you to a facial for £5, a full body massage for £6... the list goes on.

☺ *Mon–Fri, 9am–8pm*

Toni and Guy

5 Cannon Street

(0121) 631 3333

You'll have to make polite conversation with someone whose haircut instils you with no confidence in them whatsoever.

☺ *Mon–Wed & Fri, 9.30am–6.30pm; Thu, 9.30am–7.30pm; Sat, 9am–5pm*

☻ *From £36*

GYMS

Bannatyne's Health Club

42–44 Priory Queensway

(0121) 236 7789

'More than just a gym' is their tag line.

☺ *Mon, 6.30am–10pm; Tue–Fri, 6.30am–9.30pm; Sat–Sun, 10am–5pm*

☻ *Membership, from £120 per month*

LA Fitness

Unit 5, 55 Temple Row

(0121) 632 3950

Plenty of facilities to tone that muscle and shape that bum. If running on the spot isn't for you, try an aerobics class.

☺ *Mon–Thu, 6am–10pm; Fri, 6am–8pm; Sat, 9.30am–3pm*

☻ *Membership, from £55 per month*

INTERNET CAFÉS

The Studio Café

7 Cannon Street

(0121) 634 2800

You can partake of either light refreshments or a full-blown meal while you surf.

☺ *Mon–Fri, 7.30am–5.30pm; Sat, 10am–4pm*

☻ *£1.50 for 30 minutes*

The Welcome Lounge

4th Floor, The Pavilions, 38 High Street

(0121) 632 6156

Sod those dark and dingy geek retreats; here you can surf the net right in the middle of a busy food court.

☺ *Mon–Wed, 9.30am–6pm; Thu, 9.30am–7pm; Fri–Sat, 9.30am–6pm; Sun, 11am–5pm*

☻ *£1 for 30 minutes*

TRAINS

Central Trains
(0121) 634 2040

Chiltern Railways
(08456) 005 165

Trainline
www.thetrainline.com

AIRPORTS

Birmingham International Airport
(0870) 733 5511

East Midlands Airport
(0871) 919 9000

CAR RENTAL

Avis Rent-a-Car
St James House, 17 Horse Fair
(0870) 608 6318
◉ Mon–Fri, 8am–6pm; Sat, 8am–1pm
🔹 From £41/day

Alamo
18–20 Bristol Street
(0870) 400 4562
◉ Mon–Fri, 8am–6pm; Sat, 8am–1pm
🔹 From £32/day

Hertz
7 Suffolk Street, Queensway
(0870) 850 2663
◉ Mon–Fri, 8am–6pm; Sat, 9am–1pm
🔹 From £29/day

TAXIS

Atlas Cars
(0800) 977 4262
These guys will carry the world, given half a chance, and they've got cars for up to 11 people if needs be.

Castle Cars
(0121) 472 2222
Licensed private hire cars. Which is generally preferable to unlicensed, never-on-time-'cos-its-public-transport and not-for-hire.

TOA Taxis
(0121) 427 8888
Taxis On Acid? Tragic Old Animals? Topnotch Or Average? Who cares? Metered black cabs are their speciality.

Useful info

TAKEAWAYS

Adam's Place Fish and Chips

546–548, Bristol Road, Selly Oak

(0121) 472 0913

Adam's remains a fave. Good enough for us to forgive the missing 'i' in the name.

🕒 *Mon–Tue, 11.30am–12am;*
Wed–Sat, 11.30am–1am

Caspian Pizza

23 Smallbrook, Queensway

(0121) 643 7882

No matter what time you stumble in here, the staff are as cheerful as the chips they're serving are cheap. Except if you're in there to pick a fight or steal pizza. We imagine they wouldn't be so friendly then.

🕒 *Mon–Sun, 5pm–4am*

Mr Egg

22 Hurst Street

(0121) 622 4344

Legendary greasy spoon café, perfect for late night post-clubbing fish and chips, kebabs, pies and burgers. It fits in well on the edge of the gay quarter with the slogan 'Eat like a queen for £3'.

🕒 *Mon–Thu, 8am–6pm; Fri–Sat, 8am–4am*

Pizza Land

600 Bristol Road

(0121) 471 4442

Not so much a land as a small shop to be honest. Home to the famous three topping pizza for £3. The staple of many a student's diet and the beginning of the end for that trim waistline.

🕒 *Mon–Sat, 5pm–1am*

Support

West Midlands Police HQ
(0845) 113 5000
Lloyd House, Colmore Circus
www.west-midlands.police.uk

City Hospital (Accident and Emergency)
(0121) 554 3801
Dudley Road

University Medical Practice
(0121) 687 3055
5 Pritchatts Road, Edgbaston
www.theump.co.uk

NHS Walk-In Centre
(0121) 255 4500
Lower Ground Floor, Boots, 66 High Street
www.nhs.uk

University Dental Practice
(0121) 687 8882
5 Pritchatts Road, Edgbaston
www.udp.org.uk

Boots
(0121) 643 9069
102 New Street
www.boots.com

Brook Advisory Centre
(0121) 643 5341
59–65 John Bright Street
www.brooke.org.uk

Samaritans
(0121) 666 6644
13 Bow Street
www.samaritans.org.uk

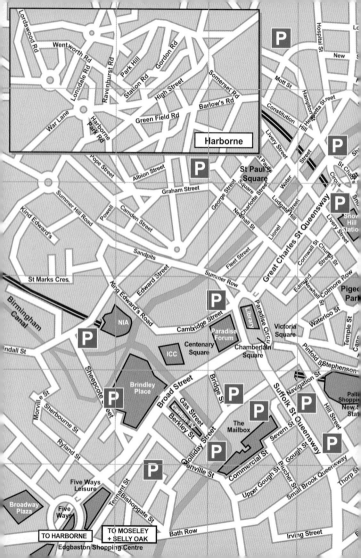

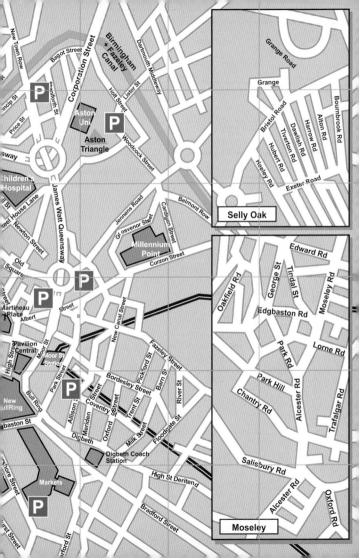

Index